"Shame is an emotion that when mishandled can significantly limit our lives and relationships. This thoughtful book offers a comprehensive road map to understanding shame and addressing its often invisible but powerful hold over us. The authors translate the robust set of skills in dialectical behavior therapy (DBT) into practical, accessible tools that can change our relationship with shame in a step-by-step fashion. Best read actively from beginning to end, it provides a clear and hopeful pathway for anyone seeking to understand and liberate themselves from the burdens of this difficult emotion. Highly recommended."

> —**Steven C. Hayes, PhD,** originator of acceptance and commitment therapy (ACT), and author of *A Liberated Mind*

"These prolific and knowledgeable authors have created a self-help workbook, using DBT skills to target shame, one of the most painful and intractable emotions. Chapman and Gratz use clear language to offer practical applications of the DBT skills, as well as providing ample clinical vignettes and engaging self-assessments and exercises to guide clients toward seeking relief from shame. I love how this book helps readers conceptualize, reduce vulnerability to, and reduce their shame."

> —**Jill Rathus, PhD,** codirector of Cognitive Behavioral Associates, NY; professor of psychology at LIU; and coauthor of *DBT Skills Manual for Adolescents* and *DBT with Suicidal Adolescents*

"The emotion of shame can be debilitating for so many people. This book gives us invaluable information, with detailed and realistic examples and worksheets for taming shame using DBT skills. Loving ourselves and realizing that we all have a place in this universe, what a beautiful gift this book is, an essential read for those who struggle with shame and for all those who love them."

> —**Lynn Courey, CSW,** founder and president of The Sashbear Foundation, helping families with skills and hope

"Shame is a painful and complex emotional experience for many people, and even more so if it is an emotion that endures. Therapists rarely focus on shame, and while many patients find therapy useful in general, for many patients shame persists even after therapy has ended. DBT experts Chapman and Gratz have delivered a step-by-step approach for addressing shame, one that will help not only those who struggle with the emotion, but one that will also provide useful ideas for therapists unfamiliar with treating the experience. Highly recommended!"

> —**Blaise Aguirre, MD,** founding medical director of 3East DBT Continuum McLean Hospital, and assistant professor in psychiatry in the Harvard Medical School department of psychiatry

"In this essential workbook, Chapman and Gratz provide step-by-step guidance on managing the painful emotion of shame. This easy-to-read text provides a compassionate framework for understanding shame, and practical tips for preventing, reducing, and effectively coping with it when it arises. This includes skills for reducing vulnerability, managing painful sensations, dealing with negative thoughts, changing unhelpful action urges, managing interpersonal consequences, and increasing self-acceptance—accompanied by clinical vignettes and practice exercises. For anyone struggling with shame—this manual is indispensable."

—**Thomas R. Lynch, PhD,** emeritus professor in the school of psychology at the University of Southampton, UK; and author of *Radically Open Dialectical Behavior Therapy*

"This book provides a long-awaited, contemporary examination of shame—offering clear explanations, practical guidance, and effective recovery strategies. It's an invaluable resource for anyone who is struggling with problematic shame, providing hope and empowerment for a healthier, more fulfilled life."

—**Shelley McMain, PhD,** senior scientist and head of the Borderline Personality Disorder Clinic at the Centre for Addiction and Mental Health, and associate professor in the department of psychiatry at the University of Toronto

"If you suffer from excessive or unwarranted shame, or are trying to help someone deal with this painful emotion, you will find few resources based on evidence-based principles or practice. In this brilliant, much-needed book, Chapman and Gratz convey in a clear, practical manner how to use skills drawn from DBT—a treatment with strong research support for treating emotional and behavioral disorders—to combat shame's devastating impact."

—**Clive J. Robins, PhD, ABPP,** professor emeritus of psychiatry and behavioral neuroscience at Duke University; and trainer and consultant at Behavioral Tech, LLC

The
Dialectical Behavior Therapy Skills Workbook *for* Shame

Powerful DBT Skills to Cope with Painful Emotions & Move Beyond Shame

Alexander L. Chapman, PhD, RPsych
Kim L. Gratz, PhD

New Harbinger Publications, Inc.

Distributed in Canada by Raincoast Books

Copyright © 2023 by Alexander L. Chapman and Kim L. Gratz
New Harbinger Publications, Inc.
5674 Shattuck Avenue
Oakland, CA 94609
www.newharbinger.com

Cover design by Amy Shoup

Acquired by Catharine Meyers

Edited by Jean Blomquist

Library of Congress Cataloging-in-Publication Data on file

Printed in the United States of America

25   24   23

10   9   8   7   6   5   4   3   2   1   First Printing

To M, I wish you peace, self-acceptance, and happiness.

—ALC

To all my patients who have struggled with shame,
I wish you peace, acceptance, and self-compassion.

—KLG

Contents

Introduction and Guide to This Book

We all struggle with shame from time to time. Shame is one of those ingredients of the human condition. We've probably all felt it, maybe even more often than we think. If you've ever found yourself avoiding talking about something because you were afraid of how others might think of you, there's a good chance that shame was involved. If you've ever wanted to hide who you are, your identity, interests, or heritage, chances are that you were feeling some shame. When we judge ourselves negatively about something, such as saying to ourselves that we're "bad," not good at something, or not as good as others, we're likely to feel shame. Further, shame is one of those emotions that creeps up on you. You don't always know you're feeling it until you find yourself avoiding people, avoiding your problems, or just feeling miserable and wondering why.

If you're reading this book, you or someone you love probably struggle with shame. If so, you probably know that shame is one of the most painful emotions a person can experience. When shame is intense and persistent, it can greatly affect the quality of your life and relationships. That's why we wanted to write a book to help people who struggle with shame break free from the hold it can have on their lives. We've both witnessed just how debilitating it can be to struggle with intense shame. Throughout our careers, we've worked with many people who struggle with shame. Some of the people we've worked with have become so swallowed up by shame that they've lost relationships, stopped engaging in activities that used to be important to them (such as going to social gatherings, engaging in exercise, or being in public), and ended up isolated and depressed. Therefore, our goal for this book is to help people learn how to cope with shame more effectively and reduce the hold it has on their lives.

In this book, we will help you understand shame and teach you effective skills for managing and coping with it. In the first few chapters, we will help you understand shame and how it differs from other emotions. We'll also discuss how skills from dialectical behavior therapy (DBT; Linehan 1993a, 2015) can help you overcome shame. We will then review DBT skills that you can use to understand your patterns of shame and what leads to shame for you, as well as to cope effectively with shame and lessen its hold on your life. By the end of this book, we hope that you

- have a clearer understanding of shame and why it arises, as well as what it feels like for you;

- can identify shame when it arises;

- know how to take care of yourself and your body so that you're less vulnerable to intense shame;

- can increase positive experiences in your life to shield you from intense shame;

- can reduce the types of negative self-judgments that often lead to shame;

- learn how to avoid getting caught up in shame-related thoughts;

- actively avoid harmful behaviors that can make things worse when you feel shame (such as self-harm, substance use, or avoiding people);

- learn to take a step back from the negative thoughts that often come along with shame;

- know how to cope effectively with shame when it arises; and

- avoid letting shame get in the way of important relationships.

Before you get started, though, we want to give you a better sense of how common shame is and why DBT skills can be so helpful for managing shame.

WHO STRUGGLES WITH SHAME?

Although there's no such thing as a "shame disorder" psychiatric condition, many mental health challenges come along with a lot of shame. People with posttraumatic stress disorder, for example, often feel shame about their past trauma or current emotional struggles that stem from such trauma. People with social anxiety often feel ashamed and humiliated in social situations (such as speaking, eating, or socializing with others), and as a result, they avoid those situations. People with eating disorders or who struggle with their weight often feel ashamed of how they look and go to great lengths to modify their appearance. People with serious and persistent mental health challenges, such as schizophrenia and bipolar disorder, often feel shame about having mental health problems. Society often judges, treats differently, or even actively rejects (that is, stigmatizes) people for having mental health challenges. People often internalize this stigma and feel ashamed for having these challenges. Others who are members of marginalized groups often feel shame about who they are, or their gender or cultural identity or heritage. Being someone who has a different identity, cultural, social, or economic background than most people around you can be very difficult, and can be a recipe for shame.

WHY DIALECTICAL BEHAVIOR THERAPY SKILLS?

You might be wondering why we're focusing on DBT skills for shame. The main reason is that we believe DBT skills can be incredibly powerful allies in your efforts to overcome shame. Indeed, DBT was developed specifically to help people who often experience considerable shame: chronically suicidal people. When Dr. Marsha Linehan, a professor at the University of Washington, was developing DBT, her aim was to help people who were experiencing intense misery. She decided she'd start with people who were chronically suicidal. Although the clients she worked with had many different problems, most of them also experienced intense shame. As a result, many of the skills and strategies that make up DBT come from work with people who struggle with shame.

Here's a little information about dialectical behavior therapy (DBT). (We expand on this topic in chapter 2.) DBT is a treatment that includes several parts:

- weekly individual therapy (usually for about an hour)

- a weekly skills-training group (usually for about two hours) in which clients can learn skills in the areas of mindfulness, emotion regulation, distress tolerance, and interpersonal effectiveness

- a therapist who is available for between-session phone calls focused on how to apply coping skills in real life

- a team approach to therapy, consisting of weekly meetings among therapists who support each other in their efforts to do the best possible work with their clients

DBT works especially well to help people manage their emotions, such as shame. DBT therapists seek to help their clients understand and manage emotions effectively. They do this by teaching them skills for responding to their emotions in helpful ways, helping them understand how their emotions might be helping them or leading them astray, and teaching them how to build meaningful relationships and avoid making stressful situations worse even when experiencing painful or intense emotions.

There is some evidence that a brief, skill-oriented DBT approach might be especially helpful for shame (Rizvi and Linehan 2005). In one of the only studies in this area, five women with borderline personality disorder (BPD, a disorder in which people often feel shame) received eight to ten sessions of a DBT-oriented treatment. The treatment involved one of the skills we're going to teach you later in this book: opposite action. This skill entails basically doing the opposite of what you feel like doing when you feel shame. People often, for example, feel like hiding themselves or avoiding others when they feel shame. Opposite action would involve seeing others and being open about the things you're ashamed of. All of the people in this study attended all planned sessions and completed the treatment as well as reported reductions in shame. This was a small study and more research is needed. Yet, it appears that a brief treatment consisting of only one of the many powerful DBT skills that we are going to teach you can make a difference when it comes to shame.

HOW TO USE THIS BOOK

Probably the most helpful way to navigate the book is to read it from start to finish. The earlier chapters offer background on shame, providing a solid foundation that makes it easier to use the skills discussed in later chapters. If you already know a fair amount about shame and your own patterns of and cues for shame, you may want to zero in on a chapter that covers the skills you need most. The summary of each chapter below should help you decide how you'd like to proceed.

- Chapter 1 covers what the field of psychology knows about shame and why it arises, as well as the different components of shame.

- Chapter 2 provides a summary of DBT and the various DBT skills covered in this book.

- Chapter 3 helps you learn how to identify and understand your own patterns of shame and what experiences lead to shame for you.

- Chapter 4 addresses ways to reduce your vulnerability to intense shame by taking care of your body and increasing positive experiences in your life.

- Chapter 5 describes how you can use DBT mindfulness skills to reduce the types of self-judgments that often lead to shame and avoid getting caught up in shame-related thoughts.

- Chapter 6 offers skills to help you avoid acting on your shame and making a stressful or difficult situation worse.

- Chapter 7 reviews skills to deal with the negative thoughts that often accompany and fuel shame.

- Chapter 8 focuses on how to use the skill of opposite action, or doing the opposite of what your shame is telling you to do, to help you reduce your shame.

- Chapter 9 discusses ways to effectively express your emotions and avoid allowing shame to get in the way of important relationships.

- The final chapter revisits many of the ideas and skills from this book and gives you some guidance on how to move forward and continue to work on building a life free from shame.

As you read the book, you'll have opportunities to reflect and answer questions about yourself and your experiences, complete helpful exercises and worksheets, and do some guided practices. The audio practices and many of the exercises and worksheets are available for download at the website for this book: http://www.newharbinger.com/49616. For more details on this, see the very back of this book.

Once you start incorporating the skills in this book into your everyday life, you'll be in a much better position to manage your shame when it arises and keep it from worsening. You'll also be able to reduce feelings of shame and its hold on your life. Understanding and effectively managing shame can make an enormous difference in your life and your relationships, helping you to get closer to important goals and to build a meaningful life. What's more, as you start to become freer from intense shame, you'll probably start to feel better and more at peace with yourself overall.

MOVING FORWARD

We look forward to sharing with you what we know about shame and how to cope with it effectively. We've witnessed just how challenging it can be to struggle with intense shame and are committed to teaching people the skills they need to break free from this painful emotion. We also have decades of experience teaching clients how to cope with and reduce their shame. This book is a wonderful opportunity to use what we've learned in our professional lives to help people recover from shame and gain more self-acceptance. The first step in learning how to cope with shame more effectively is to have a solid understanding of what shame is and why it arises. That's what we talk about in chapter 1. Let's get started!

CHAPTER 1

Everything You Need to Know About Shame and Where It Comes From

Before you can fix a problem, you need to understand that problem. That same principle applies here. Before you can learn how to manage and cope with intense shame, it's important that you understand what shame is, how it differs from other emotions, and what tends to elicit or cause shame. That's what we'll teach you in this chapter. By the end of this chapter, you should have a much better understanding of shame and where it comes from.

WHAT IS SHAME?

In a nutshell, shame is considered an unpleasant self-conscious emotion. Before we explain what exactly that means, though, it is helpful to understand what an emotion is. The first thing that's important to know is that emotions are universal. From the moment we are born, all human beings around the world have the capacity to experience a range of emotions, including anger, fear, sadness, joy, surprise, and disgust. Emotions are part of being human, and there's a very good reason we have them.

In fact, you can think about your emotions as a guide for your life. In most cases, emotions can be incredibly helpful, providing you with important information about yourself, other people, and the world around you. Emotions can help you figure out how to respond effectively to situations that arise in your daily life and alert you to the need to keep yourself safe in harmful situations. Emotions also enrich our relationships, helping us feel close to, communicate with, and understand others.

For these reasons, most of the emotions you experience can be thought of as helpful and adaptive. For example, anger may tell you that something you need or want is being blocked in some way, or that you've been violated in some way. Sadness may signal that you've experienced a loss, or are missing something that's important to you. Fear may signal danger and threat and prompt you to leave the situation. Joy may signal that you're in a situation that is rewarding and meaningful to you. All of these emotions provide important information that can guide your behaviors.

Shame, though, is different from most other emotions people experience. First, unlike the emotions we mentioned above, shame is one of a set of emotions that aren't present from birth and that people learn to experience as they grow up. Now, just because certain emotions aren't present at birth doesn't mean that those emotions aren't helpful. There are many emotions that develop later in life and yet still serve important purposes, like guilt, embarrassment, and pride. Like shame, these emotions are considered *self-conscious emotions*, in that they require both self-awareness and the ability to evaluate oneself (Lewis et al. 1989). Unpleasant self-conscious emotions in particular arise when people evaluate themselves, their behavior, and/or their personal characteristics negatively (Tangney and Tracy 2012). That's why these types of emotions develop later in life—people's sense of self and ability to reflect on themselves and evaluate their own behavior develop as they grow. However, there are important differences between shame and other unpleasant self-conscious emotions that make shame less useful, more painful, and more difficult to manage effectively.

To help you understand exactly what shame is and why it tends to not be useful, let's consider the differences between shame and guilt. As we mentioned before, both of these emotions arise when people negatively evaluate some aspect of themselves or their behavior (Tangney and Tracy 2012). *Guilt* stems from negative evaluations of specific things you did or said. For example, if you lost your temper and yelled at one of your friends, you may experience guilt. In this situation, guilt would be a helpful emotion. It would let you know that yelling at your friend isn't okay, or is not consistent with the type of person you want to be. Guilt would make you want to avoid this behavior in the future and motivate you to repair the damage to your relationship that may have been caused, such as by apologizing to your friend.

Shame, on the other hand, tends to stem from negative evaluations of yourself as a whole—and this means that the information that shame provides isn't helpful. Shame basically tells you that you are flawed, faulty, or otherwise not acceptable as you are—information that is never helpful! What's more, the message shame sends that there is something inherently wrong with you as a person can actually get in the way of changing problematic behaviors. Think about it—if you think that you're a decent person who sometimes does things that aren't okay, you may experience guilt and be motivated to work on changing behaviors that you don't like. If you think that you're just a terrible person all around, however, it's probably hard to imagine that things could ever change. When you feel shame, it's easy to believe that it's pointless to work on changing your behavior.

The table that follows will help you distinguish shame from guilt and identify when the self-conscious emotion you're experiencing is shame. (The table is available for download at http://www.newharbinger.com/49616.)

TABLE 1.1 DISTINGUISHING SHAME AND GUILT

Shame and guilt are both unpleasant self-conscious emotions that arise when someone negatively evaluates themselves or their behavior. Although people often use these terms interchangeably, there are important differences between these emotions and the best strategies for managing them effectively. This table can help you distinguish between the two.

What are you negatively evaluating?

Shame	Guilt
Myself	Something I said to someone
Who I am as a person	Something I did
Some aspect of my identity (for example, my ethnic, sexual, or gender identity)	One of my behaviors
	One of my actions

What information is this emotion providing you?

Shame	Guilt
I'm a terrible person.	I did something wrong.
There's something wrong with me.	I hurt someone I care about.
I'm flawed or faulty.	I didn't act like the type of person I want to be.
I'm not worthy.	
I'm undeserving of good things.	

What does this information make you want to do?	
Shame	**Guilt**
Avoid people or situations	Make amends or apologize
Hide	Correct a situation or mistake
Look away	Ask for forgiveness
Harm or punish yourself	Explain yourself
Beat yourself up or judge yourself	

Another key feature of shame is that it tends to have a social component. This ties into the fact that shame is a self-conscious emotion. As we mentioned before, self-conscious emotions require the ability to self-evaluate, which often means comparing oneself to others or to societal norms and expectations. For this reason, shame can often have a social component related to how we think others will perceive and respond to us. If you believe others will judge you, not accept you for who you are, or reject you, there's a good chance that you could experience shame.

UNDERSTANDING THE COMPONENTS OF SHAME

Now that you have a better sense of the type of emotion shame is and how it differs from other emotions, it's time to focus on the different components that make up shame.

To start, it's important to know that all emotions are made up of three different components: cognitive (the thoughts that go through your mind), physical (the way your body responds), and behavioral (the things you do or have urges to do). Let's take anger as an example. The cognitive component of anger may include thoughts such as *This shouldn't be happening to me! What a jerk!* or *This is so unfair!* At a physical level, feelings of anger are often accompanied by a racing heart, clenched fists, tense muscles, or a tight jaw. The behavioral component of anger may include urges to scream, throw things, or punch something or someone.

With other emotions, the physical sensations that go along with them are often the first thing you notice. For example, if you were experiencing fear, you might notice that your heart is racing, your mouth is dry, and you have butterflies in your stomach. If you noticed those sensations, you might conclude that you're feeling afraid.

The Cognitive Component of Shame

Shame is a bit different, though. Although shame also has a physical component (and we will get to that in just a moment), the cognitive component of this emotion tends to be the one that people notice first and is the best indicator that shame is present. Specifically, because shame tends to arise from negative judgments of yourself as bad, flawed, unworthy, or unacceptable in some way, these types of thoughts can be one of the clearest signs that you're struggling with shame. What's more, because these thoughts are so painful and powerful, they are often easily recognizable (and hard to ignore even if you try!). Here are some of the most common thoughts that tend to accompany feelings of shame:

- *There's something wrong with me.*

- *There's something wrong with who I am or some aspect of my identity.*

- *My thoughts, feelings, or behaviors are unacceptable.*

- *I'm a bad person.*

- *I'm not good enough.*

- *I'm flawed in some way.*

- *I'm inferior to others.*

- *I'm unacceptable.*

- *I'm unworthy or undeserving of good things.*

The Physical Component of Shame

Now, when it comes to the physical component of shame, this may not be as easily recognizable as it is for some other emotions. Shame tends to be accompanied by a range of physical sensations. Some of these sensations involve increases in arousal like you'd experience when feeling anger or fear, like feeling flushed and hot, having tightness in your chest, and having difficulty breathing. However, other sensations that go along with shame are more similar to those that accompany sadness, like a sinking feeling or stomachache. These are some of the most common sensations that go along with shame:

- sinking feeling

- pit in your stomach

- feeling hot or flushed in the face

- feeling sick to your stomach

- tunnel vision

- choking sensation or feeling like you're suffocating

- difficulty breathing

- tightness in your chest

- nausea

- heaviness in your limbs

The Behavioral Component of Shame

The final component of shame is the behavioral component, which includes what you feel like doing and what you actually do when you're experiencing shame. Let's start with the things you feel like doing when you feel shame. These are called *action urges*. A key component of any emotion is the action urge that goes along with it. The most common action urges that go along with shame are urges to hide or avoid, punish yourself, or beat yourself up or criticize yourself in some way. Although acting on these urges is usually not effective, they make sense when you consider the types of self-judgments that often lead to shame. If you evaluate yourself as terrible, flawed, and unacceptable, then punishing yourself or staying away from other people would make sense. Now, just to be clear—we don't think that these types of self-judgments or action urges are helpful, and this book will teach you all kinds of skills for reducing those judgments and acting more effectively when you're experiencing shame. However, from the point of view of understanding shame, it makes sense that those types of action urges would accompany an emotion driven by negative self-evaluations. Here are some of the specific action urges that most commonly accompany shame:

- hide, withdraw, or avoid others

- cover your face

- slump, hunch over, or make yourself small

- beat yourself up or criticize yourself

- look away or down, avert your eyes, or avoid eye contact

- punish yourself (for example, do something to hurt yourself)

- hide some of your experiences or parts of yourself from others

- apologize profusely

- ask for forgiveness repeatedly

- hide your face, turn your camera off, or only partially reveal yourself online (such as during online meetings or other events)

In addition to action urges, the behavioral component of an emotion includes the things you actually tend to do when you're experiencing that emotion. The types of actions that often accompany shame are the same as the action urges listed above. In fact, if you're struggling with intense shame, then chances are that the actions listed above are things you often do when you're experiencing shame. Take a moment to think about what you tend to do when you're experiencing shame. Write down some of your most common actions here.

_____

_____

_____

_____

WHAT CAUSES PEOPLE TO STRUGGLE WITH SHAME?

Given that shame usually isn't very helpful or adaptive, you might wonder why some people experience intense shame. That's a very good question. Although there are many factors that can contribute to struggles with shame, for many people, difficulties with shame arise from a combination of their personality and environment. Basically, if someone is hardwired to experience shame more frequently and that person is in an environment that sends them messages that they aren't acceptable or good enough, there is a good chance that person could have difficulties with shame.

So, what do we mean when we say that someone's personality can make them more vulnerable to shame? Well, research has found that people vary in a personality trait called *shame-proneness*, or the tendency to experience shame across different situations (Lewis 1971; Schoenleber and Berenbaum 2012; Tangney et al. 1992; Tangney and Dearing 2002). You may have noticed this yourself. Perhaps you've noticed that some people you know don't seem to feel shame very often, even if they are in situations that could be embarrassing or where they're told that something they did isn't okay. These people would be considered low in shame-proneness. Even in situations that could elicit shame in many people, they just don't tend to feel shame. Alternatively, there are some people who tend to experience shame quite a bit: those people are high in shame-proneness. For these folks, it can feel like shame is a go-to emotional response a lot of the time. If there are any cues for shame present, then they will probably experience shame, at least to some degree. Take a moment to think about the trait of shame-proneness and how it applies to you. Do you tend to experience shame across a number of different situations? Or are your feelings of shame limited to only select situations and experiences? Write down your reflections here:

_____

_____

_____

_____

Of course, being high in shame-proneness in and of itself does not mean that someone will struggle with intense shame. Instead, there are certain environments that are more likely to intensify feelings of shame: specifically, environments that send a message that you or something about yourself is unacceptable or not good enough. Now, when we're talking about the environment, it's important to know that this can refer to your immediate environment, like your family or close friends, or to the broader environment in which you live, like your community or even society as a whole. The key is that either specific people or society as a whole tell you that you aren't good enough or are flawed in some way. If that's the message you're receiving from those around you, then it's no wonder that you would struggle with shame.

As we discussed earlier, shame tends to arise when you judge yourself as bad, flawed, unworthy, or unacceptable. Although these types of negative self-judgments can come from within yourself, they often stem from or are reinforced by similar types of messages from others. Therefore, if you grew up in a family, community, or society that told you that you or something about yourself wasn't acceptable, it would make a lot of sense if you struggled with self-judgments or came to believe that there was something wrong with who you are. In fact, research has found that it's common for people to *internalize* the negative beliefs and judgments of others (especially if these are pervasive), or start to believe these negative messages about themselves (Drapalski et al. 2013; Simbayi et al. 2007; Waugh, Bryne, and Nicholas 2014; West et al. 2011). And these internalized negative beliefs about the self can be particularly damaging to one's self-worth (Lysaker, Roe, and Yanos 2006; Rössler 2016) and especially likely to lead to shame (Schoenleber and Berenbaum 2012).

Social Stigma and Marginalization

When it comes to negative messages from your community or society as a whole, it's important to consider the role of social stigma and marginalization, as these can explain why some people struggle with shame. *Stigma* is associating negative qualities with someone simply because that person has a particular characteristic, such as a mental health difficulty, physical disability, physical illness, or particular sexual or ethnic identity. For example, research has found that people who struggle with mental health problems often face considerable social stigma, and may be viewed by society as dangerous or unpredictable (Rössler 2016). In addition to leading to negative perceptions of any person with that characteristic, stigma can lead to discrimination and marginalization—which are very relevant to experiences of shame. As we mentioned in the introduction to this book, people who are members of marginalized groups can feel shame about who they are or some aspect of their identity.

Marginalized groups are people who have historically been treated negatively by society as a result of some aspect of themselves or their identity, like their cultural or ethnic background, sexual or gender identity, or disability status. For example, members of a marginalized group may not have the same access to opportunities or resources as other people, or may be targets of unfair treatment or even violence. When someone is a member of a marginalized group, they are inundated with messages from society that they are "less than" or not as important as other people. These messages tend to be pervasive—they are difficult to escape. People from marginalized groups often encounter these messages from other people or society as a whole on a daily basis, and these types of messages can influence how they perceive themselves. Think about it: If you're constantly exposed to messages that you, as a person, are not good enough or are flawed in some way, it can be very difficult not to internalize those negative messages. When these messages are internalized, which is called *internalized stigma*, people are much more likely to buy into the idea that there is something inherently wrong with them, leading to shame.

Traumatic Experiences

Another environmental factor that can be a major source of shame is traumatic experiences. Traumatic events, especially the experience of sexual or physical assault, can drastically change the way you see the world, other people, and yourself. Humans tend to believe that the world is generally a safe place, people are generally good, and people have control over their own bodies, safety, and well-being. When someone experiences a traumatic event, these perceptions of the world, others, and themselves are shattered, and they are left trying to make sense of what occurred. The problem is that it is usually incredibly difficult, if not impossible, to understand or figure out why someone would hurt someone else or why terrible things can happen to people. As a result, in an attempt to make sense of the traumatic experience, people may begin to blame themselves—*It must have been due to something I did,* or *If I had just made a different choice, then this wouldn't have happened to me,* or even *If this happened, I must have deserved it.* Although these types of thoughts are distressing, they can give the illusion of control and make people think that there is something they can do to prevent such an event from happening again. Even if you have to blame yourself, having an explanation for what happened and the sense that you may be able to prevent it in the future can feel better than not being able to understand or make sense of what occurred. The problem, though, is that these types of thoughts are typically not an accurate reflection of events and can lead to intense feelings of shame.

What's more, not sharing these types of traumatic experiences with others, or actively hiding them from others, can further intensify shame. Especially in cases of sexual or physical assault, people often don't want others to know about what happened (probably because of the shame they're experiencing). If you've experienced a traumatic event, you might feel uncomfortable talking about it with other people, or may even go out of your way to hide this from others. Although this is understandable (as sharing what happened to you can bring up painful thoughts and emotions, or you may be scared about how others will react), actively hiding a part of your history can sometimes send the message that there is something wrong or shameful about your history—basically, that some part of your history must be hidden. This can then intensify feelings of shame. Finally, because traumatic events can be so hard to overcome or cope with, you may feel "damaged," "unlovable," or "helpless"— negative self-perceptions that can provide a breeding ground for shame.

Take a moment to reflect on what you've learned about the environmental factors that can lead to shame. Are any of these factors relevant to you? Think about the messages you've received from your environment and any experiences you've had that may have led to or intensified feelings of shame for you. Write down your thoughts here:

_____

_____

_____

_____

_____

SPECIFIC CUES FOR SHAME

Now that you have a better understanding of why some people are simply more prone to experiencing shame, it's time to turn our attention to the types of experiences or situations that can elicit shame in the moment. Although it may seem like your shame is almost always present regardless of what's going on, it's important to keep in mind that emotions are always *cued*, or brought about by, something in the moment. Even if it seems like some emotions just come out of the blue or are always there, they are always cued by something. Shame is no different.

So, what types of experiences tend to elicit or cue feelings of shame? Well, not surprisingly, they are similar to the types of experiences that can make someone more prone to experiencing shame in general. Specifically, most cues for shame involve either direct messages or the perception that you're unacceptable, not good enough, or have failed in some way. If you think back about the types of environments that can make people more prone to struggling with intense shame, this probably makes a lot of sense. The environments most likely to put someone at risk for struggling with shame are those that tell people they aren't good enough, or that there's something wrong with them. Therefore, if you encounter cues like this in your daily life, it makes sense that they'd bring up shame. Being told that you or something about yourself, like your feelings, beliefs, or an aspect of your identity, is unacceptable in some way is one of the most common cues for shame. It'd be hard to get that message and not experience at least some shame. So, being around people who criticize you, tell you that what you believe or feel isn't acceptable, or are just not accepting of you or some aspect of your identity is likely to cue shame for many people.

Now, as we noted above, cues for shame can involve either direct messages that you or something about yourself is unacceptable in some way, or just the perception that you're unacceptable. This distinction is important, because it means that sometimes shame can arise even without a message from someone else that you aren't acceptable as you are. Instead, if you've internalized these messages or have a tendency to judge yourself negatively, these negative self-judgments and criticisms can elicit shame in the moment. In fact, this is one reason why some people can feel as if shame is almost always present: if criticisms and negative judgments of yourself for perceived failures or wrongdoings, or even just for who you are, can elicit feelings of shame, then this means that you could be surrounded by cues for shame much of the time. The good news, though, is that if a lot of your cues for shame are internal (or cues that come from within yourself), that means that you can learn ways of responding to these cues more effectively and reducing the extent to which they elicit shame. A lot of the skills we'll be teaching you in this book will help with that, and will provide powerful strategies for changing the way you respond to some of the most common cues for shame.

In chapter 3, we're going to help you identify the experiences and situations that tend to cue shame for you. For now, though, these are some of the most common cues for shame:

- spending time with people who are not supportive of you

- being told that you did something wrong

- being told that a part of you or your identity is not okay

- being told that something you believe or feel is wrong or unacceptable

- being criticized, yelled at, or made fun of by someone

- being criticized or ridiculed in front of other people

- being rejected by others for something you did, thought, or felt

- doing something that goes against your values or who you want to be as a person (for example, something that hurts someone else)

- doing something others have told you is wrong or bad

- making a mistake or failing at something

- being reminded of something you did in the past that you are not proud of

- having something you don't like about yourself exposed to others

MOVING FORWARD

If you've been struggling with shame for a while, changing patterns of shame and reducing the hold it has on your life will take some time. Although we are confident that the skills you learn from this book will help you move past your shame, recovering from shame is a process that takes time. Therefore, the goal of this book is to teach you as many skills as possible for preventing shame, managing shame when it arises, and not getting caught up in shame in the same way as you may have done in the past.

CHAPTER 2

Overview of DBT and the DBT Skills

Amanda showed up at her therapist's office ten minutes late, feeling anxious and overwhelmed. Her friend had suggested that she meet with a DBT therapist because she seemed so down about herself and appeared depressed. Although Amanda trusted her friend and decided to make an appointment, she had not heard of DBT and had no idea what to expect.

During her first session, Amanda's therapist asked Amanda questions about her life, her background, her current experiences and symptoms, and her history of suicide attempts. The therapist seemed comfortable talking about these things and was upfront, direct, and warm. Amanda had been struggling with a low mood and really negative thoughts about herself, her appearance, and where she was in her life. She was avoiding friends and starting to feel more isolated. Amanda read a blog about someone struggling with shame who described similar experiences: avoiding people, judging herself, and feeling isolated. She raised this with her therapist, and it soon became clear that shame had been casting a shadow on Amanda's life for quite some time.

In this chapter, we will periodically return to the example of Amanda to illustrate what it's like for someone learning DBT skills for shame. Along the way, we will provide an overview of DBT, followed by a description of the DBT skills. We will start by describing what DBT is and how and why DBT was developed. We will then describe the four sets of skills we teach people in DBT and how they can be helpful in managing shame in particular.

A BRIEF HISTORY OF DBT

Dr. Marsha Linehan, who struggled with serious mental health challenges, developed DBT. Dr. Linehan, a professor emeritus at the University of Washington and a psychologist, began to develop DBT in the 1970s. You'll notice that we refer to Dr. Linehan as "Marsha" as one of us has worked closely with her, and she has said to call her "Marsha" instead of "Dr. Linehan" when we talk about her. In any case, earlier in her life, Marsha experienced serious mental health problems, engaged in self-injury and suicidal behavior, and had psychotic symptoms (hallucinations, delusions). As a teenager and young adult, Marsha was hospitalized in a psychiatric institution. She's even shared that, at one point, staff considered her to be their most severely mentally ill patient (Linehan 2020).

During Marsha's experiences on her path to recovery, she began to realize that she wanted to help people like herself. She used to talk about how she had been in hell and wanted to teach others how to get out of hell. Her aim was to find people who were experiencing intense misery and help them learn to build lives that would bring them joy and make their lives worth living. Marsha reasoned that some of the people who were probably experiencing the most intense misery were those who tried to end their lives. As a result, when DBT was first developed, the focus was on helping chronically suicidal people learn skills for reducing their suffering and finding their way in life. DBT has now become a treatment that can be helpful for people with a variety of concerns, such as borderline personality disorder, self-harm, anger, depression, posttraumatic stress, and certain eating disorders, among others.

One way to help people learn to build lives that are worth living is to help them change life circumstances, thoughts, and actions that lead to emotional suffering, such as shame. In Amanda's case, for example, she felt shame about many areas of her life, such as her work, relationships, and appearance. Therapy might help her work on dissatisfaction about her job situation, reduce her judgments about her appearance, and stop avoiding or isolating herself from others.

One of the first steps in overcoming shame is to understand its effect on your life. As this book is about shame, you might want to consider what's leading to shame in your life. Check the boxes of all the things you struggle with currently. Consider the checklist below, which includes several statements that are common among people who experience a lot of shame. Check off the ones that apply to you.

☐ Are you experiencing shame-related feelings that are painful or overwhelming on a regular basis?

☐ Do you feel tormented by negative thoughts about yourself, who you are, or what you do or have done?

☐ Do you have the thought that there's something wrong with you or that you're a bad person?

☐ Have you had traumatic or stressful experiences in the past that are affecting you now? Do you ever blame yourself for these experiences or feel too ashamed to talk about them? Do you find yourself avoiding people or situations out of a sense of shame?

☐ Do other people treat you negatively or seem to judge or reject you?

☐ Do you sometimes feel different or like an outsider?

☐ Are you not doing enough things that are meaningful or important to you because of shame?

☐ Are you coping with shame by engaging in actions that might help in the short term but make things worse in the long term, such as self-harm, drug or alcohol use?

How many of these statements have you checked off? Even if it's just a few, shame might be playing a pretty negative role in your life. The good news is that, by checking off the difficulties you experience related to shame, you've taking an important step—clarifying some of the things that would have to change for you to become freer from shame.

THE NEED FOR CHANGE

In our lives, we all have many sources of stress and, at times, misery. One way to overcome this misery is to try to make changes in our lives and build lives that we enjoy and find meaningful. This is the ultimate goal of DBT: to help people learn how to build a life worth living. As it turns out, doing so involves making a lot of changes, and that's not easy! To overcome the misery of shame, we often have to change our behavior and our perspective, learn new coping skills, relate differently to the people around us, ask people to treat us differently, and so on. Needing to change some things about your behavior or your life doesn't mean that you're the cause of your own problems. In fact, in DBT, the assumption is that people don't cause their own problems. At the same time, it is up to each of us to find a way to solve them.

THE NEED FOR ACCEPTANCE

One of the most important ideas in DBT, though, is the acknowledgment that change is not enough. While developing DBT, Marsha quickly learned that as important as it is to help clients change the aspects of their life that are causing suffering, clients also need to learn to accept themselves as they are.

This is because the only way to change your life is to first accept the way things are. Let's say you had a serious illness, such as cancer. If you refused to accept your diagnosis, ignored your symptoms, and avoided medical appointments, you'd be in big trouble. Instead, as hard as it would be, if you were to acknowledge and accept that you have cancer, you'd probably be more likely to seek appropriate care and treatment and have a much better chance of recovering.

The same thing applies when it comes to recovering from emotional suffering, traumatic or stressful circumstances, or other life difficulties: you can't change your life without first accepting that it is the way it is. Shame, unfortunately, often makes people want to do the opposite of accepting their problems; it makes them want to avoid their problems. Have you ever noticed that, when you feel ashamed, you want to hide, avoid thinking about your problems, and avoid opening up to others? It's hard to solve problems that you're avoiding. If you feel ashamed about being depressed and not doing things you'd like to do with your life, an important first step is to acknowledge and accept that your life isn't the way you want it to be. You might also acknowledge and accept that you feel a sense of shame that makes you feel miserable and gets in your way. If you were to accept these problems, you'd probably be more likely to help yourself and seek help from others than you would if you were to avoid them. Therefore, to overcome shame, you have to both accept the way things are and work toward changing things. Fortunately, that's the whole point of DBT and DBT skills.

To learn more about acceptance, Marsha decided to visit a monastery during a sabbatical from her work as a professor. During her three months there, Marsha learned about Zen practice, which simply involves paying attention to what you are experiencing in the present moment. (For more information about Zen and mindfulness, see Shunryu Suzuki's *Zen Mind, Beginner's Mind*). To do this, we often have to let go of what we want and experience what we have. We might want to move, scratch an itch, find a better chair to sit in, run from the room screaming, eat different food, and so on. While practicing Zen and mindfulness, the idea is to simply experience all of these desires, avoid acting on them, and stay focused on the present moment.

Marsha recognized that these essential skills of being mindful of the present and accepting things as they are were crucial for her clients, who had experienced so much pain and suffering and had tremendous difficulty accepting things as they are. DBT came to include a set of skills called *mindfulness skills* as well as the skill of *radical acceptance* (we'll describe these more soon). As such, in addition to solving the problems that are making you miserable, DBT can also help you become more mindful and attentive to your present-moment experience and accept things as they are.

Learning about DBT mindfulness and acceptance skills can teach you how to accept many important things. If you struggle with shame, you probably sometimes have a hard time accepting yourself or characteristics of yourself. You might also have a hard time accepting things that have happened to you or things you've done in the past. It's also not uncommon to have difficulty even accepting that you feel shame or other challenging emotions. DBT skills can help you to accept all of these difficult parts of your life, while also moving forward to make important changes and build a life that you're happy with. Complete the following exercise 2.1 (or download the exercise at http://www.newharbinger.com/49616).

Exercise 2.1: Things You're Having a Hard Time Accepting

In the spaces below, please describe things you're having a hard time accepting in three areas of your life.

1. Yourself or characteristics of yourself that are hard to accept:

   Amanda's example: I'm having a hard time accepting that I weigh more than I'd like to.

   _____

   _____

   _____

2. Current life circumstances or situations that are hard to accept:

   Amanda's example: I'm having a hard time accepting that I have a low-paying job when friends with the same education seem to be more successful.

   _____

   _____

   _____

3. Shame or other emotions that are hard to accept:

   Amanda's example: I'm having a hard time accepting that I feel so sad and ashamed so often. It's really painful.

   _____

   _____

   _____

Now that you've completed exercise 2.1, you have a better idea of areas of your life that are hard to accept. DBT skills can help you move toward accepting these areas. Once you do that, you'll probably experience less emotional suffering and less shame. Shame is an example of your mind telling you that there is something wrong with you or that you are not okay in some kind of fundamental way. Basically, shame tells people that something about themselves and who they are as a person, like their personality, identity, or other characteristics, is bad or unacceptable. Therefore, learning to accept yourself, your life circumstances, and who you are can be an ideal way to help you start chipping away at shame. Let's take a look at how shame works in Amanda's daily struggle. You'll continue to read more about Amanda's DBT therapy as the chapter progresses.

Amanda's Story

Amanda arrived at her therapy session feeling down, having had a terrible day the previous day. She had felt miserable, high levels of shame, and had self-harmed. She and her therapist worked together to try to figure out what happened. Amanda had been hanging out with a friend, had too much to drink, started comparing herself and her appearance to that of her friend, and then felt envious, inadequate, and ashamed. Once the shame overcame her, she didn't know what to do to get out of it, so she left the get-together early and tried to distract herself with a TV show at home. When this didn't work, she became angry and frustrated with herself, which further intensified her shame. Feeling at her wit's end, she harmed herself as a way to feel better and punish herself for being "bad." Once she and her therapist figured out how this all had happened, they discussed skills Amanda could have used that may have made things go differently.

THE NUTS AND BOLTS OF DBT AND LEARNING DBT SKILLS

What are the components of DBT? Although this workbook is about DBT skills to help you with shame, it's important for you to know that DBT is a broader treatment that doesn't just involve skills. DBT is what we call a "comprehensive treatment," as it includes many components designed to help people with complex psychological or emotional problems. You might not be in a DBT program, but in case this treatment is of interest to you, these are the different parts of it:

- **Individual therapy**, involving meeting weekly with a therapist to work on goals that are important to you, reduce behaviors that are getting in your way (such as self-injury, substance use, avoidance, or other behaviors), and build the life that you want.

- **Telephone consultation**, involving your individual therapist being available by phone (or email, text, etc.) between sessions to help you use the skills you're learning in therapy in difficult, everyday life situations.

- **Skills training group**, involving a weekly group in which you learn all of the DBT skills (discussed further below).

- **A DBT therapist consultation team**, involving a team of therapists who all meet weekly to make sure they're providing effective treatment to their clients.

If you're wondering where or how to pursue comprehensive DBT treatment, there are a few steps you can take:

1. Look at the following website for the DBT-Linehan Board of Certification: https://dbt-lbc .org/index.php?page=101167. This is the organization that certifies therapists in DBT. When a therapist is certified, this means they have demonstrated skills and knowledge in the area of DBT, so you can be more confident that they know what they're doing. This website includes a list of therapists and programs that are certified.

2. Visit the website for Behavioral Tech, LLC: https://behavioraltech.org/. Behavioral Tech is the company that Marsha founded to train therapists in DBT. The Resources section of the site includes a list of teams/programs that have received their intensive training in DBT.

3. Visit the website for your local state, provincial, or other organization for psychologists, social workers, or counselors. Often, these websites have referral directories, and you might be able to search for a therapist who does DBT. This doesn't mean that the therapist you find will offer comprehensive DBT services, but you can ask them about that when you reach out to them.

THE DBT SKILLS AND HOW THEY CAN HELP WITH SHAME

DBT includes four sets of skills to help people learn how to build lives that are worth living. The idea in DBT is that many of us have not had the chance to develop the tools we need to build happier and more fulfilling lives. In some cases, maybe you never learned these things when you were younger. Perhaps negative life events, such as abuse or trauma, made life really difficult for you, making it harder to learn how to cope. For some, particular characteristics or tendencies, such as being a really impulsive person who often acts on the spur of the moment without thinking or being a highly emotional person, could get in the way. If you're a really emotional or impulsive person, coping is more complicated. You have to learn how to understand and manage your emotions and stop yourself from doing things that get you in trouble. For whatever reason, perhaps you haven't learned some of the skills that might have helped you experience less misery and shame. The good news is that it's never too late!

The four sets of skills in DBT include mindfulness, distress tolerance, emotion regulation, and interpersonal effectiveness skills. Here are descriptions of these skills and how they can help with shame.

Mindfulness Skills

As we mentioned earlier, mindfulness and acceptance skills are probably among the most helpful ways to deal with shame. Shame, by definition, often involves nonacceptance of yourself. In contrast, *mindfulness skills* involve experiencing and accepting reality as it is. DBT mindfulness skills involve strategies to help you learn to experience and participate in life in the present moment. You'll learn to access your "wise mind," which is like intuition, taking into account your emotions and your thinking. You'll also learn to notice and experience the present moment through your five senses. This is so you can label and accurately describe your experiences to yourself and others. Then you'll be able to participate or immerse yourself in important activities in the present moment. You'll also learn to be nonjudgmental toward yourself and others, to focus on one thing at a time, and to do what works to deal with problems in your life.

Mindfulness skills are especially helpful for shame. These skills can help with shame in the following ways:

- identify and name the emotion of shame when it occurs

- learn to step back from shame, avoid acting on it, and do what is most helpful

- learn to approach yourself, your emotions, and your experiences without judgment

- take a step back from the negative thoughts about yourself that often accompany shame and approach these thoughts in a different way.

Amanda and her therapist discussed some of the skills she could have used to make the other night go differently. Amanda suggested that she could start with mindfully describing how she was feeling and the thoughts that were going through her mind. For example, when she was feeling envious and judging herself negatively, Amanda could have practiced the mindfulness skills of observing and describing how she was feeling in a nonjudgmental way, then labeling her self-judgments as just thoughts her mind was having. For example: I feel envious that my friend seems more fit and healthy than I, has a job that I'd like, and has a partner. This makes sense because I am still working on improving my life, and it is normal to want these types of things. Although I don't like feeling this way, I do feel this way and that is okay. The judgmental thoughts I am having about myself are just thoughts—not facts. It is just something my mind is telling me. However, I don't need to buy into these thoughts.

Distress Tolerance Skills

DBT *distress tolerance skills* include two main categories of skills: crisis survival strategies and reality acceptance skills. *Crisis survival strategies* are there to help you avoid making things worse when you're in a crisis or stressful situation; they include distraction, self-soothing, managing extremely intense emotions effectively, and other skills. *Reality acceptance skills* help you to accept things as they are. Some of these skills include radical acceptance, which involves acknowledging and accepting things as they are in the present moment. Reality acceptance skills include turning the mind, which involves committing to yourself to accept whatever you're experiencing. Another skill is willingness, or accepting things as they are and doing what works.

Distress tolerance skills can help you

- avoid doing things that make your situation worse when you feel shame;

- get a little break or breather from your feelings or judgmental thoughts;

- accept yourself, your emotions, your experiences (both past and present); and

- move forward effectively in dealing with shame.

When Amanda learned about the skill of radical acceptance, she immediately thought that this could be an ideal skill for reducing her shame. Thinking about the night when she had harmed herself, she realized that one of the problems had been that she had a really hard time tolerating her feelings of envy. When she experienced those feelings, she beat herself up for feeling that way and judged herself as dumb and inadequate. This meant that she didn't just have to cope with the pain of feeling envy, but the additional suffering that came from beating herself up and feeling ashamed with herself for feeling envy. And this, in turn, made things so much worse. Practicing radical acceptance could have helped her reduce suffering and prevent some of her feelings of shame.

Emotion Regulation Skills

DBT *emotion regulation skills* help you learn to understand, identify, and manage your emotions. Some of these skills will help you learn to understand what emotions are, why we have them, and how they can help us (or get in our way sometimes). You will also learn to accurately describe and label your emotions, such as shame, anger, fear, sadness, and other emotions. Other skills will help you change what you do when you feel strong emotions, how you think about situations that bring up strong emotions, and how you can solve problems that lead to strong emotions. Finally, emotion regulation skills also include strategies to make you less vulnerable to stress and strong emotions. These strategies involve taking care of your body and mind, practicing coping ahead of time with stressful situations, and building more positive and meaningful experiences into your life.

Emotion regulation skills can help with shame in these ways:

- better understand shame, why you're experiencing it, and what you can do about it

- approach the negative thoughts about yourself that often accompany shame in a different way by focusing on evidence that contradicts self-judgmental and self-berating thoughts

- act in a way that fits your values, even if you feel shame

- act in a way that goes against shame, such as by being open with others and being kind to yourself

- decrease your vulnerability to intense shame and solve some of the problems that might be contributing to shame

Later that night, when shame about her body and about having a hard time functioning in jobs started to creep in, Amanda could have identified and labeled her emotion as shame rather than just acting on the feeling and the self-judgmental thoughts. Just taking a step back from the emotion would have given her the space to identify other skills that may have helped her lessen her shame. For example, instead of harming herself, she could have decided to be kind to herself by engaging in self-soothing strategies, which are part of the distress tolerance skills. She could also have used the emotion regulation skill of checking the facts to reframe judgmental thinking patterns that were feeding her shame and making it worse. And rather than getting caught up in judgmental thoughts—like What's wrong with me that I can't do these things? Why can't I just eat better and stick to an exercise routine? I can't do anything!—Amanda could have focused on the facts by saying to herself, I'm disappointed about how things are. It's frustrating that things are so hard for me. It makes sense that I'd be frustrated. It is understandable that I'd want things to be different and better. However, struggling with these things doesn't make me a bad person or mean that there is something wrong with me. I'm not the only one with these challenges. A lot of people struggle with health, weight, and work. Punishing myself will just make things worse and make me feel worse about myself.

Interpersonal Effectiveness Skills

In DBT, we view *interpersonal effectiveness* as the ability to get your needs met while maintaining important relationships. It's not always easy to do this, particularly if you're prone to shame. If you feel a lot of shame, for example, you might not consider your needs to be important. You might avoid asking for what you want or need from others, instead prioritizing others' needs. When this happens, you might feel bad about yourself, as you're not making your needs important, and your relationships can suffer as well.

There are several DBT interpersonal effectiveness skills. One of the first sets of skills involves learning to identify your goals in your relationships so that you can meet these goals while maintaining the relationship and your self-respect. Other skills involve learning to ask for what you want and need, and also saying no to things you don't want to do in ways that are positive for your relationships and help you feel good about yourself. Additionally, some of these skills will help you figure out when, how, and whether to ask for things from others (such as whether to ask for a favor or for someone to treat you differently), or to say no to what others are asking of you. Finally, other skills involve learning how to identify and leave destructive relationships, build new ones, and recover from invalidating statements that others sometimes make.

Interpersonal effectiveness skills can help with shame in these ways:

- find ways to communicate effectively to people even when you feel shame

- ask people to change their behavior when part of the problem contributing to shame is the way others are treating you

- say no to requests to do things that just increase your shame or reduce your self-respect

- identify relationships that might need to change, or that you might want to reconsider, particularly if shame is a big part of those relationships

- learn to recover from or address things other people say, without ending up in a shame spiral

When she was hanging out with her close friend, Amanda could have used interpersonal effectiveness skills to open up to her friend about how she was feeling. She could have described the emotions coming up within her, such as envy when her friend was talking about how good her life was, while also conveying respect and caring for her friend. She could, for example, have said something like, "Hearing about this new job, I feel a little torn. On the one hand, I feel happy for you. I care about you, and you've worked so hard and you really deserve all of this success. On the other hand, I feel like I'm still struggling so much. I can't even get myself out of the house some days. To be honest, I feel a little envious. So, it's bittersweet to hear how well things are going for you. It's not that I don't want to hear about the good things in your life, but I figured I should just be open with you about all of this because we're such good friends." Being open goes against the grain of shame, which makes us feel like concealing or hiding our feelings. Also, having a supportive discussion with her friend could have forestalled the shame spiral that occurred later. Shame often has to do with being rejected by others, but if Amanda were to experience acceptance from her friend, this could have dampened the shame.

MOVING FORWARD

To help people suffering from serious and complex mental health challenges, Dr. Marsha Linehan developed DBT. She realized that effective treatment requires a balance of acceptance and change. DBT is a broader, cognitive-behavioral treatment that includes individual therapy, telephone consultation, skills training, and a therapist consultation team (as we briefly described). Importantly for the purposes of this book, DBT includes four sets of skills: mindfulness, distress tolerance, emotion regulation, and interpersonal effectiveness. All of these skills can be used to help manage feelings of shame and begin to break the hold shame has on your life. We look forward to teaching you these skills throughout the rest of this workbook, and we're confident that you will find them to be powerful allies in your journey toward experiencing freedom from shame.

CHAPTER 3

Understanding Your Patterns of Shame

In order to cope with any painful or difficult emotion, you first need to recognize that you're experiencing the emotion. Only then can you use skills to manage it effectively. Thus, when it comes to managing feelings of shame, it's essential to better understand your own patterns of shame, including what tends to lead to shame for you and what shame feels like for you. The more you understand your own patterns, the better able you'll be to use the skills you learn in this book to manage your shame, or even prevent it from occurring.

IDENTIFYING CUES FOR YOUR SHAME

Just like all emotions you experience, an emotion of shame is always *cued*, or brought about, by something. Even if it feels like your shame sometimes comes out of the blue or is just always present, all emotions are cued by something. That's just the way emotions work.

However, that doesn't mean that it's always easy to figure out the cues for shame. Especially if your shame is chronic and long-lasting, it might seem like nothing in particular brings it about in the moment; instead, it might seem like it's just always present regardless of what's going on. In addition, some cues for shame are internal cues, or cues that come from within yourself, like your thoughts, emotions, memories, or bodily sensations. Therefore, if you aren't fully aware of all aspects of your internal experience, or if you're focused on aspects of your experience outside of yourself (like your interactions or the situation you're in), these cues can be difficult to identify or notice.

The good news, though, is that even though identifying shame cues in the moment can be challenging, many people who struggle with shame find that the situations and experiences that tend to cue their shame are tied together by a smaller number of common themes. And once they identify these themes, they can predict when they're most likely to experience shame.

As we discussed in chapter 1, although there are many different types of experiences that can elicit feelings of shame, most cues for shame involve messages that you're not good enough or have failed in some way. These messages can range from very subtle suggestions to clear and direct statements that you or something about you is unacceptable (such as when someone tells you that there is something wrong with an aspect of your identity, or that you should not feel or act a certain way). Sometimes these messages will be intentional; other times, the other person might not intend to be sending this message at all, and might even be upset if they realized that's how it was interpreted (for example, if someone gives you constructive feedback about something you could improve but doesn't suggest or imply that you would have been expected to do it differently before the feedback). These messages can also just come from yourself, such as when you criticize yourself for a perceived failure or wrongdoing. Yet, although messages that you're not good enough or have failed are common cues for shame, everyone has their own unique shame cues. Therefore, it's important to figure out what is most likely to bring up shame for you. Exercise 3.1 can help you with this. (You can download this exercise at http://www.newharbinger.com/49616.)

Exercise 3.1: Identifying Cues for Your Feelings of Shame

Close your eyes and take a few minutes to think about the types of situations and experiences that tend to bring up shame for you. What situations, experiences, interactions, or thoughts tend to cue your shame? Think about times you've experienced shame recently and what was going on at that time.

The following list contains common cues for shame. Place a check mark next to all that apply to you.

☐ Being reminded of a past traumatic event

☐ Spending time with people who are not supportive of you

☐ Doing something that hurts or upsets someone else

☐ Doing something that goes against your values or who you want to be as a person

☐ Doing something others have told you is wrong or bad

☐ Being made fun of by someone

☐ Failing at something

☐ Being told that you did something wrong

☐ Being told that a part of you or your identity is not okay

☐ Being rejected by others for something you did, thought, or felt

☐ Being reminded of something you did in the past that you are not proud of

☐   Having something private or personal exposed to others

☐   Having something you don't like about yourself exposed to others

☐   Being criticized or yelled at in front of others

☐   Being told that something you believe or feel is wrong or unacceptable

☐   Making a mistake

Are there other situations or experiences that tend to bring up shame for you? List them on the lines below.

_____

_____

_____

_____

_____

Knowing the types of situations and experiences that tend to bring up feelings of shame for you is an important step in learning to manage your shame. If you know when you are most likely to experience shame, you can plan ahead for how to cope with feelings of shame that may arise in these situations. Basically, knowing the times you're most at risk for experiencing shame will allow you to identify the skills you can use to manage these feelings ahead of time, when it is easier to plan and think clearly. In DBT, we call this *coping ahead*. You can think of it as similar to planning a road trip to a new place. If you have a good map and take the time to plan ahead, you will know the roads to take, which turns to make, and even where you can stop for lunch, gas, and so on. Because you've taken the time to plan the trip beforehand, you'll be in a much better position to navigate the roads without getting lost. If, on the other hand, you were to set out on a road trip to a new place with no plan, you might find yourself lost, panicking, or having a hard time figuring out what to do next. Coping with shame is similar: if you can see shame on the horizon and plan ahead for how to cope with it effectively, you'll be in a much better position to manage it when it arises.

Another reason it can be important to understand the cues for shame is that you might be able to avoid or at least limit your exposure to some of these cues. For many of the emotions people experience, it isn't possible to avoid all of the situations that bring up those emotions; they are just a natural part of being human and living one's life. For example, it isn't possible to avoid all situations that make you angry, everything you're afraid of, or all experiences, memories, or thoughts that bring up sadness. And this is the case for some shame cues as well; some of these experiences are just a normal and expected part of life. However, some of the shame cues you identified may be avoidable to at least some extent. For example, if there are particular people in your life who disapprove of some aspect of your identity or tend to tell you that who you are or the things you do, feel, or think are not acceptable, you could consider limiting contact with those people to limit your contact with those shame cues. Although it may not be possible to avoid them completely (and you may not even want to do so), you could think about ways to limit the amount of time you spend with them or to avoid seeing them when you are feeling more vulnerable to shame (something we'll discuss in chapter 4).

Sam's Story

Sam always thought that they were very aware of their patterns of shame and what shame felt like for them. It was hard to go a day without being painfully aware of all of their negative self-judgments and thoughts that they were unacceptable, unlovable, and a failure. It certainly seemed like Sam was aware of these thoughts and related urges to avoid others and keep to themselves on a daily basis.

When Sam's therapist asked them to spend some time identifying the types of situations and experiences that tended to bring up feelings of shame for them, Sam was hesitant. What was the point of focusing on all of the things that caused them shame? When their therapist suggested that understanding patterns of shame was the first step in learning how to manage shame, Sam decided it was worth a try.

Initially, thinking through the various things that caused them shame was painful, and they had to schedule breaks to make the exercise more tolerable. The more they worked on the exercise, though, the more they realized that there were patterns to their shame cues that they hadn't been aware of before, and some common cues that seemed to account for a lot of their shame.

One of these cues was getting feedback at work. Sam noticed that receiving any kind of negative feedback (even if this was accompanied by feedback on things they were doing well) almost always caused a sinking feeling in the pit of their stomach and urges to avoid interacting with the person who gave them the feedback, as well as thoughts that they were an idiot or a failure. Knowing this, Sam came up with a plan for how to cope with shame that may arise at work and how to take care of themselves on days when feedback could be expected.

Sam also realized that another high-risk situation for shame was spending time with their mother, who was not accepting of Sam's gender identity. Whenever Sam spent time with their mother, thoughts of being unacceptable and unlovable increased, and Sam found it harder to work up the motivation to go out with friends and not isolate at home. After realizing this, Sam decided to spend less time with their mother until they had more practice using different skills for managing shame. After a few weeks of limiting calls and visits with their mother, Sam noticed that their shame wasn't as frequent or intense as it had been before.

RECOGNIZING AND IDENTIFYING FEELINGS OF SHAME

Now that you have a better understanding of the types of experiences that tend to bring up shame for you, the next step is to become more aware of how shame feels for you. The sooner you can recognize feelings of shame, the sooner you can use the skills you learn in this book to help you cope with and manage those feelings.

As you may remember from chapter 1, all emotions are made up of three components: physical (the way your body responds when you experience an emotion), cognitive (the thoughts that go along with the emotion), and behavioral (the things you do or have urges to do when you experience an emotion). Identifying the different components of your shame and becoming more aware of each one will make it easier to recognize your shame sooner (Linehan 1993b, 2015).

Fortunately, DBT has some very helpful skills for recognizing and identifying your emotions that will help you become more aware of your shame and how it feels in your body. One of the most helpful is the skill of mindfully attending to your experience without getting caught up in the experience (Linehan 1993b, 2015). Rather than getting caught up in or consumed by your shame, the goal of this skill is to just notice all the different parts of your emotion without pushing them away or clinging to them. Simply pay attention to the physical sensations, thoughts, and action urges that go along with shame, watching each of these experiences arise and pass from one moment to the next.

To start, it may be helpful to bring your attention to how the shame feels in your body and the different sensations you're experiencing (for example, a feeling of heat in your face, heaviness in your limbs, or sinking feeling in your stomach). Then, bring your attention to the thoughts that are present and any urges you're experiencing to act in some way. If you find yourself getting caught up in your thoughts or desires to act in a certain way, gently turn your attention back to how the shame feels in your body. As you notice each component of your emotion, be sure to take an objective and neutral stance. Focus on just noticing each sensation, thought, or urge as it is (for example, a feeling of heat in my face, a feeling of sinking in my stomach, a thought that *I'm not good enough*, an urge to hide) without pushing it away or getting caught up in it.

One way to begin practicing this skill is to think about a recent time you experienced shame and try to reconnect with what that emotion felt like in the moment. Exercise 3.2 provides simple step-by-step instructions for mindfully attending to the components of your shame without getting caught up in those experiences. To access guided audio instructions, visit http://www.newharbinger.com /49616.

Exercise 3.2: Mindfully Attending to Different Components of Your Shame

1. Find a comfortable and quiet place where you can sit or lie down.

2. Close your eyes.

3. Focus on your breathing. Notice what it feels like to breathe in and breathe out. Notice what parts of your body move as you breathe in and out.

4. Think about a recent time when you felt shame at a moderate level of intensity. Try to focus on a time when your shame was around a 4 or 5 on a scale from 0 to 10, where 0 equals no emotion and 10 equals the most intense emotion possible. Focus on this experience and try to get a clear picture of it in your mind.

5. Bring your attention to your body and notice where in your body you feel the shame. Scan your body from head to toe, paying attention to any sensations in your head, neck, shoulders, back, chest, abdomen, arms, hands, legs, and feet. Spend about ten seconds on each area of your body, stepping back in your mind and just paying attention to and noticing the sensations.

6. Once you have finished scanning your body, bring your attention to the parts of your body where you feel shame. Zero in on these sensations. Watch them rise and fall in your mind's eye as you would watch a wave rise and fall in the ocean.

7. If you begin to get caught up in the sensations, notice that, and then bring your attention back to noticing the sensations as just sensations.

8. Bring your attention to any thoughts that are present, focusing on just noticing these thoughts as thoughts without attaching to them. If you find yourself getting caught up in your thoughts, notice that, and then bring your attention back to just noticing the thoughts that are present.

9. See if you can bring your attention to any action urges you are experiencing. Focus on just noticing these action urges as they rise and fall, bringing attention to the ways they change or stay the same.

10. Keep focusing on the different components of your shame without escaping or avoiding them. Continue to just notice your sensations, thoughts, and action urges without trying to push them away or change them. Do this for about ten to fifteen minutes, or until the emotion subsides and you no longer feel shame.

INCREASING YOUR AWARENESS OF THE DIFFERENT COMPONENTS OF SHAME

Now that you have practiced mindfully attending to your shame without getting caught up in it, it's time to identify the different components of your shame. As we mentioned earlier, all emotions are made up of three different components: physical, cognitive, and behavioral. Becoming more aware of each component will make it easier for you to recognize and identify feelings of shame.

Physical Component

Because emotions are full-body responses, the physical sensations and bodily changes that go along with an emotion can be some of the earliest signs that you're experiencing an emotion. What these sensations feel like depends on the emotion you're having, as different emotions are associated with different physical sensations.

Shame in particular involves a mix of different types of physical sensations. Unlike some other emotions that mostly involve either increases in arousal (for example, anger and fear) or decreases in arousal (for example, sadness), shame involves both increases and decreases in arousal and activation (Nummenmaa et al. 2013). This means that shame can sometimes be more challenging to identify than those other emotions, because you need to be aware of more physical sensations at one time to know that you're feeling shame. The good news, though, is that the physical sensations that tend to go along with shame are, together, relatively unique to this emotion. Use exercise 3.3 to help you identify the physical sensations that tend to go along with shame for you.

Exercise 3.3: Identifying the Physical Sensations Associated with Shame

Close your eyes and focus on what shame feels like for you. What does shame feel like in your body? What physical sensations tend to go along with feelings of shame for you? Place a check mark next to all of the physical sensations associated with shame for you.

☐ Sinking feeling   ☐ Hot, red face

☐ Pit in your stomach   ☐ Choking sensation

☐ Feeling hot   ☐ Feeling like you're suffocating

☐ Feeling flushed   ☐ Difficulty breathing

☐ Feeling sick to your stomach   ☐ Tightness in your chest

☐ Tunnel vision   ☐ Slumped shoulders

☐ Blushing   ☐ Nausea

Are there other physical sensations that tend to go along with feelings of shame for you that were not listed above? If so, please list those on the lines below.

_____

_____

_____

_____

Cognitive Component

As we discussed in chapter 1, one of the main causes of shame is negative self-judgments, or evaluating oneself as bad, flawed, unworthy, or unacceptable. Although all emotions have a cognitive component, this component is more prominent in shame than in some other emotions. For example, it's possible to experience fear without having any thoughts go through your mind. If there's a loud or unexpected noise, you might just have a fear response without even evaluating what that noise means or whether it's dangerous. Likewise, seeing your beloved pet do something cute can elicit feelings of joy and love without any thoughts or interpretations of that event being present.

Shame is different, however. It's rare to experience shame without some type of judgment or evaluation of yourself as flawed, bad, or unacceptable in some way. Thus, one of the clearest signs of shame, and one of the easiest to recognize for many people, is the negative self-judgments that accompany this emotion. When you notice these thoughts, there's a good chance that you're experiencing shame. In fact, the presence or absence of these types of thoughts can help explain why some people who make a mistake, hurt someone's feelings, fail at a task, or receive criticism experience shame and others do not. You're much less likely to experience shame if you don't judge yourself for these experiences. For example, if you approached these experiences as regrettable and yet human, natural, and understandable, they'd be much less likely to elicit shame. Shame tends to arise when people interpret these types of experiences to mean that they are unworthy or unacceptable.

For these reasons, it is incredibly important to identify the specific thoughts and judgments that tend to accompany shame for you. This will help you identify your shame sooner and be more aware of how your interpretations of different events and experiences can actually intensify shame. Exercise 3.4 will help you identify the specific thoughts that tend to accompany feelings of shame for you.

Exercise 3.4: Identifying the Thoughts That Go Along with Shame

Think about the thoughts that tend to go along with shame for you. What kinds of thoughts and interpretations accompany feelings of shame for you? Are there particular thoughts that tend to be present when you're experiencing shame? Place a check mark next to all of the thoughts associated with shame for you.

- ☐ Thinking that there's something wrong with you or some aspect of your identity
- ☐ Thinking that there's something wrong with your thoughts, feelings, or behaviors
- ☐ Thinking that you're a bad person
- ☐ Thinking that you aren't good enough
- ☐ Thinking that you're to blame for something bad happening
- ☐ Thinking that you're flawed in some way
- ☐ Thinking that you've done something that isn't acceptable
- ☐ Thinking that you've failed at something or haven't met someone's expectations
- ☐ Thinking that your feelings or beliefs are silly or stupid
- ☐ Judging yourself as inferior, unacceptable, or not good enough
- ☐ Judging yourself as unworthy in some way
- ☐ Thinking that you are unlovable
- ☐ Thinking you've done something wrong

Are there other thoughts that often go through your mind when you're experiencing shame that were not listed above? If so, please list those on the lines below.

_____

_____

_____

_____

Behavioral Component

Sometimes the first component of an emotion that people notice is the behavioral component. This component includes the things you feel like doing and the things you actually do when you're experiencing shame. Even before you notice your physical sensations or the self-judgments going through your mind, you might be aware of your urges to do something or to act in a certain way. For example, some people find that the first clue that they're experiencing shame is the urge to harm themselves, beat themselves up, or hide from others. If the behavioral component of shame is also the first one you tend to notice, then knowing how this emotion makes you want to act could be a helpful strategy for recognizing feelings of shame sooner.

So, when you experience shame, what do you want to do? What action urges do you experience? Do you have an urge to act in a certain way? Do you want to hide or withdraw or criticize yourself? Use exercise 3.5 to help you identify the action urges that go along with feelings of shame for you.

Exercise 3.5: Identifying the Action Urges That Go Along with Shame

Think about the things you want to say or do when you're experiencing shame. What kinds of action urges go along with shame for you? What does shame make you want to do or say? On the list below, place a check mark next to all of the action urges that go along with shame for you.

☐ Hide

☐ Cover your face

☐ Beat yourself up

☐ Criticize yourself

☐ Look away

☐ Look down

☐ Avert your eyes

☐ Punish yourself

☐ Do something to hurt yourself

☐ Say mean things to yourself

☐ Hide some of your experiences from others

☐ Avoid eye contact

☐ Hide parts of yourself from other people

☐ Put your head in your hands

☐ Withdraw

☐ Avoid other people

☐ Speak softly

☐ Apologize profusely

☐ Ask for forgiveness

Are there other action urges that often go along with shame for you? If so, please list those on the lines below.

_____

_____

_____

_____

Now that you've identified the action urges that often accompany feelings of shame, the next step is to think about the types of things you actually do when you feel shame. How do you tend to act when you feel shame? Although a lot of the things you do when you're experiencing shame may overlap with the action urges you identified, this won't be the case for all of them. There may be some things you have urges to do when you're feeling shame that you don't actually do. For example, you may want to avoid others, but not be in a position where you can. Or, you may have urges to hide, but not allow yourself to act on those because you know that won't be helpful in the long run. Identifying the things you tend to do when you're experiencing shame and the ways in which those actions are similar to or different from your action urges will provide you with helpful information for identifying feelings of shame.

What's more, this exercise may even highlight your strengths and some skills you already have for managing shame. Specifically, if there are certain action urges for shame that you experience but don't allow yourself to act on, this may mean that you already have some skills you can rely on to help you manage your shame. Choosing not to act on shame action urges can help counter some of the messages that shame sends and keep your feelings of shame from escalating even more. What's more, not allowing yourself to act on these action urges is similar to one of the most helpful skills DBT offers for dealing with shame: the skill of *opposite action* (which we'll teach you in chapter 8). Although that skill involves doing the opposite of your action urge, just choosing not to act on an action urge can also be helpful. Therefore, even though the action urges and actions associated with shame for you may be quite similar, it's still very important to identify both behavioral components of shame. Use exercise 3.6 to help you identify the things you tend to do when you're experiencing shame.

Exercise 3.6: Identifying the Actions That Go Along with Shame

Think about the things you tend to do when you're experiencing shame. How do you tend to act? Mark all of the actions that tend to go along with shame for you.

- ☐ Hide
- ☐ Cover your face
- ☐ Beat yourself up
- ☐ Criticize yourself
- ☐ Look away
- ☐ Look down
- ☐ Avert your eyes
- ☐ Punish yourself
- ☐ Do something to hurt yourself
- ☐ Say mean things to yourself

- ☐ Hide some of your experiences from others
- ☐ Avoid eye contact
- ☐ Hide parts of yourself from other people
- ☐ Put your head in your hands
- ☐ Withdraw
- ☐ Avoid other people
- ☐ Speak softly
- ☐ Apologize profusely
- ☐ Ask for forgiveness

Are there other things you often do when you're experiencing shame? If so, please list those on the lines below.

_____

_____

_____

_____

Now that you've completed these exercises, take a moment to think about what you've learned about your personal experience of shame and what it feels like for you. How does shame tend to feel in your body? What kinds of thoughts tend to go along with shame for you? Do you tend to act on all of the action urges that accompany shame, or are there some urges that you never or rarely act on?

Reflect on what you've learned from these exercises. This will help you better recognize shame the next time you experience it.

_____

_____

_____

_____

_____

_____

_____

_____

RECOGNIZING SHAME IN THE MOMENT

Now that you have a better understanding of the different components of shame, it's time to focus on recognizing shame sooner when you experience it. Although thinking back to times you've felt shame in the past can provide a lot of useful information about how you experience shame, you may not have been paying attention to all three of the components of shame we reviewed here, or you may have forgotten some of the experiences. One of the best ways to improve your awareness of shame in the moment and your ability to recognize it sooner is to monitor your shame as it occurs in the moment. This process will help you become more aware of the bodily sensations, thoughts, action urges, and actions that go along with shame for you. And doing these exercises now, after you've learned about the three components of shame and have a better sense of what this emotion feels like for you, will put you in a better position to recognize each of its components as your emotion unfolds.

Worksheet 3.1 will help you monitor your shame on a daily basis. You can download it at http:/www.newharbinger.com/49616. We recommend printing several copies of this worksheet so that you can complete it each time you experience shame. After writing down the day and time at the top of the worksheet, try to identify the situation that led to your shame. Use the DBT skill of nonjudgmentally labeling your experience (Linehan 1993b, 2015) to describe the situation without judgment, just sticking to the facts of what happened. You'll learn more about this skill in chapter 5. Next, see if you can identify the bodily sensations, thoughts, and action urges associated with your feelings of shame. Focus on noticing each of these experiences and writing down everything you observe. Finally, write down what you did in response to the shame, or the actions you took.

Keep these monitoring forms with you throughout the day, and fill them out as soon as you can after you notice you're experiencing shame. Monitoring your shame in the moment will provide the most helpful information about your own patterns of shame and what this emotion feels like for you.

Worksheet 3.1: Monitoring Shame

Day and Time: _____

Situation: _____

_____

_____

_____

Bodily Sensations	Thoughts	Action Urges	Actions

MOVING FORWARD

The goal of this chapter was to help you become more aware of your experience and patterns of shame. In order to manage an emotion effectively, you need to be able to recognize that emotion when you're experiencing it. It's difficult to cope with an emotion if you aren't aware that you're experiencing it, or don't know what emotion you're experiencing. Understanding your patterns of shame and becoming more aware of shame as it arises will pave the way for you to use the skills you learn in the rest of this book to manage your shame effectively. Like many challenges in life, you have to understand and recognize your shame before you can work on addressing it. Therefore, as you move on to the next chapters in this book and learn more about other DBT skills that can help you cope with and reduce your shame, we encourage you to continue to practice the skills you learned in this chapter to further increase your awareness and understanding of this emotion.

Now that you have a better understanding of your patterns of shame, it's time to turn our attention to skills you can use to manage and cope with shame. The next chapter focuses on skills for reducing your vulnerability to intense shame. These skills can help you feel shame less often and less intensely, which will make it easier to manage your shame when it arises.

CHAPTER 4

Reducing Your Vulnerability
to Intense Shame

Now that you have a better understanding of what shame is, what it feels like for you, and the types of experiences that often bring about shame, it's time to focus on specific skills you can use to combat shame. Although it may be hard to imagine a life without intense shame, DBT has several powerful skills that can be incredibly helpful in reducing shame and lessening its hold on your life. In fact, one of the benefits of DBT is that it includes skills for regulating emotions at various stages of an emotion, from before you even have an emotion to when it is really intense. Having so many stages where you can apply the skills you learn means that there are many more opportunities to free yourself from intense shame.

It probably won't surprise you that the best place to start is at the earliest stages of the emotion process—before you even experience intense shame. Therefore, this chapter focuses on DBT skills to reduce your vulnerability to experiencing intense shame. These skills can help you feel shame less often or less intensely, which will make it easier to manage your shame when it arises.

TAKING CARE OF YOURSELF

The first set of DBT skills for reducing vulnerability to intense emotions involves taking care of yourself and your body. Here's the basic idea behind these skills: taking care of yourself physically makes you far more able to manage your emotions effectively and might even make your emotions less intense overall. Think about a time when you didn't feel well or weren't taking care of yourself. Perhaps you had a cold, were too busy to eat well, or hadn't slept well in a few nights. Now, think about how you felt emotionally during that time. Were you on edge? Did your emotions feel more overwhelming than usual? Did you find yourself close to tears or wanting to hide under the covers? As human beings, when we aren't taking care of our bodies, our emotions can feel a lot more overwhelming and be harder to manage. On the other hand, when we take care of our bodies, we have more resources available to manage our emotions. Therefore, a great place to start when you want to manage painful emotions is to do everything you can to take care of your body so that you are in the best position possible to manage your emotions.

Taking care of yourself physically has particular benefits if you're a person who struggles with intense shame. Taking care of yourself is basically the opposite of what shame makes you feel like doing. As we discussed in chapter 3, shame often makes people feel like neglecting themselves, being mean to themselves, or punishing themselves—all of which are the opposite of taking care of yourself. Therefore, taking care of your body can counter shame by teaching you that you are worthy of care and compassion. We will tell you a lot more about the importance of this in chapter 8 when we talk about using the emotion regulation skill of opposite action to reduce shame. What you need to know now, though, is that one way to combat shame is to do the opposite of what shame is telling you to do. So, think about these skills as a road map to a new way of treating yourself and beginning to learn that, despite what your shame tries to tell you, you deserve care and compassion.

Take Care of Illnesses

One way to take care of yourself is to do what you can to prevent illness and address any illnesses you do experience as soon as you can (Linehan 1993b, 2015). Being ill can take a real toll on your body and make it that much harder to manage emotions. When you're ill, your body tends to use all available resources to fight the illness. Although this is helpful when your body needs to recover, it doesn't leave you with many resources for managing painful emotions. And, when it comes to an emotion as intense and painful as shame, it's really important to have as many resources at your disposal as possible.

Therefore, it is really important that you take care of yourself when you are ill or feel yourself coming down with something. If you think you may be getting sick, go to the doctor and get the help you need. If you are prescribed medications for physical illness or mental health concerns, be sure to take them as prescribed. If you are struggling with a physical illness, go easy on yourself and take extra care of your body. Get extra sleep and drink a lot of liquids. Take a day off from work or give yourself a break on daily chores. Basically, do everything you can to take care of that illness and restore your physical health. You will be in a much better position to manage your shame if you are physically healthy.

Nourish Your Body with a Healthy Diet

Another way to take care of your body is to nourish it with a healthy diet full of the nutrients it needs to function at its best (Linehan 1993b, 2015). This means making sure to eat a balanced diet with plenty of nutritious fruits, vegetables, whole grains, and proteins. These are the food groups that will provide your body with the nutrients you need to lessen your vulnerability to shame and manage it more effectively when it arises. You can think of nutritious food as the fuel your body needs to regulate emotions.

When it comes to a healthy diet, it is important to ensure that your body is getting the nutrients it needs. However, this doesn't mean that you need to give up your favorite junk food or guilty pleasure entirely. It is perfectly fine to incorporate some comfort foods into your diet now and then, and to splurge with your favorite treat on occasion. In fact, if you use the DBT mindfulness skills of nonjudgmentally observing or participating when eating these types of foods, doing so can be another way of acting opposite to the urges associated with shame by doing something to care for or comfort yourself. Just make sure that you get some nutrient-rich food into your diet each day too!

Get Sufficient Good-Quality Sleep

In the same way that your body needs nutrients to function at its best, it also needs enough sleep (Linehan 1993b, 2015). Although how sleep works to help keep us healthy is still a topic of debate, sleep seems to help our brains and bodies recover from the activities of the day. When we have enough good-quality sleep, we are likely to have the resources and energy we need to face the ups and downs of the next day. If your sleep is disrupted in some way, you might find it much harder to manage your emotions, including shame. Now, getting enough sleep can be easier said than done, especially if you tend to ruminate or worry when you are in bed. However, there are a number of steps you can take to improve your sleep (Bourne 1995; Epstein et al. 2009; Linehan 2015).

Figure out your "sleep window." Oftentimes, the first step toward improving your sleep is to figure out your "sleep window." Your *sleep window* is the period when you're likely to get the most restorative sleep. If you're a night owl, maybe that's between midnight and 8 a.m. If you're an early bird, it could be between 9 p.m. and 5 a.m. You'll probably get the most restorative sleep if you sleep in a way that fits your biological clock, or *circadian rhythm*. If you don't know when you're most likely to get the best sleep, keep track of when you go to bed and get up for a week or two, along with your mood and energy level each day. You might start to notice that you feel more energetic and in a better mood on days after you've slept during particular times (for example, when you are in bed by 11 p.m. and up by 7 a.m.).

Stick to a regular sleep schedule. Once you know your sleep window, the next step is to go to bed at roughly the same time each night and get up at the same time each day. It's most important to get up at the same time every day. Doing so allows your body to develop enough "sleep drive" during the day that you'll be sleepy when it's time to go to bed at night. Although you should try to go to bed around the same time every night, it's best to wait until you feel sleepy before going to bed. If you try to force yourself to sleep when you're not sleepy, your sleep will probably suffer. Sticking to this kind of sleep schedule allows your body to get into a rhythm and learn when it is time to sleep. Eventually, this should help your body learn when to sleep and wake. Because it can take a bit of time for your body to settle into this pattern, it is best to avoid naps during the day, as this can make it far more difficult to fall asleep at night. It is also important to be patient with yourself during this process, and not to expect your sleep pattern to change overnight. The good news is that being patient with yourself can also be a way of acting opposite to the action urges that go along with shame, so this is just another opportunity to practice this skill!

Time your meals. Eat your last meal a few hours before bedtime. Although it's not helpful to go to bed hungry, it's also best not to eat right before you go to bed. It's important to give your body time to digest the meal before you go to bed.

Time your exercise routine. It's important to avoid engaging in vigorous exercise within six hours of bedtime. Exercise can increase your energy and activation and make it harder to fall asleep. Therefore, it is best to exercise in the morning or afternoon. That said, many people find it helpful to take a short, relaxing walk or engage in light exercise in the evening. It's mainly vigorous exercise you need to be careful about.

Limit your caffeine intake during the day and avoid caffeine at night. This includes foods that have caffeine, such as chocolate. Not only can caffeine interfere with your ability to sleep, it takes a surprisingly long time to leave your body. In fact, it can take five to six hours for your body to process half the caffeine from a cup of coffee. If you struggle to fall asleep at night, or if you know that you are sensitive to caffeine, it may be best to avoid caffeine entirely and see if that helps you fall asleep more easily at night.

Limit your nicotine and alcohol intake. It can be helpful to limit these substances during the day and especially when it's close to your bedtime. You may be surprised to learn that both nicotine and alcohol actually increase arousal and can interfere with sleep. Although some people find smoking a cigarette or having a drink to be relaxing, the effects of these substances on your body are quite the opposite: nicotine is a stimulant and alcohol can increase your heart rate and overall arousal. Alcohol can also interfere with slow-wave sleep, the deep sleep you need to restore your body physically. Therefore, smoking and drinking alcohol can interfere with your sleep, making it harder to both fall asleep and sleep soundly and deeply during the night.

Make your bedroom as relaxing and comfortable as possible. You want to train your brain to see your bedroom as a place to relax and sleep. When you go to bed, try to have your room at a cool temperature and ensure that it is dark and quiet. It can also be very helpful to limit possible sources of distraction or stress in this room. For example, consider removing televisions, smartphones, or computers from your bedroom if possible so that you can begin to associate this room with only sleeping. In fact, one of us (ALC) has opted to use an old-fashioned analog alarm clock so that there is no need to even bring his smartphone into the bedroom at night. Likewise, try not to do work in your bedroom. If you share a living space with others and your bedroom also functions as your office, then consider setting up the space so that there are two separate sections of the room and you don't work from bed. For an added benefit and another way of reducing shame, take steps to make your bed as comforting and soothing as possible. For example, put on very soft sheets or warm, comfy blankets. Add extra pillows to your bed and make sure they have the firmness you prefer. Making sure your bed is comfortable and cozy can be another way of treating yourself with care and kindness.

Remember that trying to force yourself to fall asleep will not work. If it was as easy as that, we wouldn't have so many skills for helping people improve their sleep! Because sleep isn't something any of us can completely control, it is incredibly important to remember that improving your sleep is a process that takes time. Therefore, even if you do everything we recommend here, you may still have difficulty falling asleep at night, particularly when you are just starting to make these changes to your sleep routine. The key is to be patient with yourself and to not beat yourself up if you have trouble falling asleep. Instead, if you find that you are still awake after being in bed for twenty to thirty minutes, get up and find something quiet and relaxing to do, such as meditating or reading a book. Keep in mind that the goal is to return to bed as soon as you start to feel drowsy, so choose something that is calming and can be stopped at any time.

As you start to make these changes, remember that developing healthier sleep patterns is a process. Changing your sleep habits isn't going to occur overnight, so don't get discouraged if you don't see immediate improvements in your sleep. The important thing is to commit to making changes and to be patient with yourself throughout this process.

Exercise Regularly

This probably won't come as a surprise to you, but exercising regularly is another very helpful strategy for reducing your vulnerability to intense emotions (Linehan 1993b, 2015) such as shame. Not only can regular exercise build up your physical resources by making your body stronger, it can make you feel better about yourself and improve your confidence and self-esteem—all of which can put you in a better position for managing any shame cues you encounter and reducing your vulnerability for shame in particular. If you feel better about yourself, it will be easier to combat any feelings of shame you experience.

So, what do we mean by regular exercise? The key is to aim for thirty minutes of some sort of moderate physical activity at least five days a week. The good news is that this physical activity can take a number of different forms, so there are many ways to incorporate exercise into your daily routine. The only requirement is that whatever you do gets your heart rate up; beyond that, there is a lot of flexibility. Although some people find it helpful to set aside time to go to the gym or an exercise class several times a week, others find that it works better for them to focus on getting moderate activity anywhere they can throughout the day so that they can incorporate it more seamlessly into their daily lives. For example, if you are going to a store or restaurant, park as far away as possible from the entrance so that you can get in a bit of a walk. If you live or work in a multistory building, take the stairs rather than the elevator. If you can, consider walking or biking to work rather than driving. If you clean your house, focus on making that process as physically active as possible by vacuuming vigorously or scrubbing the floors by hand.

To reduce your vulnerability for intense shame in particular, consider choosing forms of exercise that involve acting in ways that are opposite to what shame prompts you to do. Because shame often makes people feel like hiding from or avoiding others, helpful forms of exercise could involve setting up walking dates with friends, joining an exercise group or dance class, or participating in team sports—anything that allows you to interact with and obtain support from others.

Limit Alcohol and Drugs

Alcohol and drugs can have a major impact on your body, influencing your arousal, heart rate, and overall functioning. Alcohol and drugs can also drain your body's physical resources, leaving you with fewer resources to manage shame or respond effectively to shame cues. In addition, although alcohol and drugs can provide temporary relief from painful emotions in the short term, they tend to increase vulnerability to intense emotions in the long term by increasing distress and making it more difficult to manage emotions. Finally, because these substances lower inhibitions, alcohol and drugs can also lead to more impulsive behaviors, greater conflict, and poorer decision making—all of which could increase feelings of shame, particularly if you regret the way you behaved while under the influence. For these reasons, limiting your intake of alcohol and drugs can be a helpful strategy for reducing your vulnerability to intense shame (Linehan 1993b, 2015).

Elizabeth's Story

Elizabeth felt terrible once again. She was so run-down and exhausted, and she could feel a cold coming on. She also noticed that she was being far more critical of herself and seemed to be almost constantly beating herself up for even small mistakes or just being alive. She realized that when she didn't feel well, she was much more vulnerable to falling into old patterns of criticizing and being mean to herself. She just didn't have the energy to combat these patterns when she felt under the weather.

Although in that moment she didn't feel like she deserved care and compassion, she decided to act as if she was deserving of care by taking steps to take care of herself. To start, she decided to go to bed early and try to get a good night's sleep. When she woke up the next morning, she noticed she felt a little better and a little more regulated. Next, she decided to start her day with a healthy and comforting meal to try to nourish her body and combat her cold. She made herself a big fruit salad and had a nice bowl of oatmeal with a large glass of juice chock-full of vitamin C. When she got home from work, she made herself her favorite pasta meal and then went to bed early again.

The next morning, she started to see a difference. She felt less tired and a bit less overwhelmed. She also noticed that it was easier for her to take a step back from self-critical thoughts rather than getting caught up in them. Seeing this, she made a commitment to continue to care for herself even when she didn't really want to so that it would be easier to manage her feelings of shame.

Now that you've learned about the different skills you can use to take care of yourself physically, use exercise 4.1 to identify ways you can reduce your vulnerability to shame by taking better care of your body. (You can download this exercise at http://www.newharbinger.com/49616.)

Exercise 4.1: Reducing Your Vulnerability to Intense Shame by Taking Care of Your Body

How well are you currently taking care of yourself? The goal of this exercise is to help you identify steps you can take to improve your physical health and self-care. If you are already doing some of these activities, take a moment to congratulate yourself for treating your body with love and care. These are great ways to begin combating shame and teaching yourself that you are deserving of care.

If you aren't doing some of these activities, or if there are additional things you could be doing to care for yourself even more, think of specific actions you can take to improve your physical health in these areas. Begin by identifying three specific actions you can take to better care for yourself in each area. Taking these steps will ensure you are in the best position possible to manage shame cues and reduce your shame.

Activity	Please Circle One	Actions You Can Take to Improve Your Health
Do you go to the doctor for regular checkups?	Yes No	1. 2. 3.
Do you go to the doctor when you feel sick?	Yes No	1. 2. 3.

Activity	Please Circle One	Actions You Can Take to Improve Your Health
Do you take your medications as prescribed?	Yes No	1. 2. 3.
Do you eat fruits, vegetables, whole grains, and protein?	Yes No	1. 2. 3.
Do you focus on incorporating nutritious food into your diet every day?	Yes No	1. 2. 3.
Do you limit junk food and sweets?	Yes No	1. 2. 3.
Do you get at least seven to nine hours of sleep per night?	Yes No	1. 2. 3.
Do you have a regular sleep schedule?	Yes No	1. 2. 3.

Activity	Please Circle One	Actions You Can Take to Improve Your Health
Is your bedroom comfortable and relaxing?	Yes No	1. 2. 3.
Do you do some sort of physical activity every day?	Yes No	1. 2. 3.
Do you exercise for at least thirty minutes five days a week?	Yes No	1. 2. 3.
Do you limit your alcohol intake?	Yes No	1. 2. 3.
Do you limit your use of drugs?	Yes No	1. 2. 3.

INCREASING POSITIVE EXPERIENCES

Another set of skills that can be especially helpful for reducing vulnerability to intense shame involves incorporating more positive experiences into your life so that you can connect with more positive emotions and feel better overall. The idea behind this set of skills is that the more positive experiences you have in your life, the better position you'll be in to cope with intense negative emotions such as shame. In general, it can be easier to manage intense negative emotions when it doesn't feel like those are the only emotions you experience. When your life is enjoyable and meaningful and you're experiencing more positive emotions, you have more resources available to cope with any painful emotions that may arise.

What's more, just as with the first set of skills we discussed, incorporating more positive experiences into your life can have the added benefit of countering shame directly by teaching you that you are worthy of positive things in life. As we discussed previously, shame often arises when people judge themselves as flawed, faulty, or unworthy. Therefore, shame can send the message that you're not worthy of anything positive in life and don't deserve to do things that are fun, pleasurable, or enjoyable. This is one of the reasons why shame is so painful and debilitating. It robs people of the joy in their lives and makes them feel as if they are unworthy of anything positive. Although this is one of the most painful aspects of shame, it also provides a powerful opportunity for combating shame by counteracting these messages and incorporating more positive experiences into your life. Even if you don't feel like you deserve positive experiences, you can still build more of these into your life and reap the benefits of doing so. By incorporating more positive experiences into your life on a daily basis, you teach yourself that it is okay to have these experiences and, over time, that you are worthy of these experiences. This can help chip away at your vulnerability to intense shame.

Thus, even if you're having a hard time stepping back from shame-related thoughts and connecting to the fact that you're worthy of positive things in life, use these skills to incorporate more positive experiences into your life. Over time, increasing positive experiences in your life will help counteract the messages your shame sends and reduce your vulnerability to shame. Basically, this set of skills is all about giving yourself permission to incorporate positive activities into your life and to really connect with any positive emotions you experience as a result. Think of this as a prescription for managing shame: as doctors, we are telling you to begin to incorporate fun, enjoyable, meaningful, and overall positive experiences into your life.

When it comes to increasing positive experiences in life, this can involve three broad types of activities: pleasurable or fun activities, mastery activities, and meaningful activities. We will discuss each of these in turn.

Identifying Pleasurable Activities

The first set of activities is quite straightforward: activities that you find fun, enjoyable, or pleasurable. These activities can range from small everyday activities like cuddling with a pet, watching the sunset, or sitting outside in warm weather, to more complex and time-intensive activities like traveling, going out with friends, or going for a hike. When it comes to incorporating more pleasurable activities into your life, the first step is to identify activities that you might enjoy. Although this might sound simple, it is incredibly important. If shame has interfered with doing nice things for yourself or reinforced the idea that you don't deserve pleasure or enjoyment, then you might not even know what types of things bring you pleasure. And that's okay. Figuring out the types of activities that bring you pleasure and joy is one of the skills in DBT and can even be enjoyable in and of itself. Think of it as an expedition to learn more about yourself and what makes you happy.

One way to do this is to think about whether certain activities that many people find pleasurable could be pleasurable for you. You don't need to know for sure, and sometimes figuring out what will bring you enjoyment involves a lot of trial and error. However, reviewing the list of activities that some people find pleasurable in exercise 4.2 can be a helpful place to start. As you review this list, consider if the activity stands out to you as something you may enjoy or that could be worth trying. You can also think about whether there were any times in your life when you enjoyed these activities, even if you haven't done them in a while. The goal isn't to know exactly what activities will be best for you, but to identify ones that you'd like to try and that might be enjoyable. Place a check mark next to any you think might be enjoyable to you. We've also included some blank lines at the bottom of the table so that you can write in some of your own potentially pleasurable activities that you'd like to try.

Exercise 4.2: Identifying Possible Pleasurable Activities

Activities That Might Be Fun or Enjoyable	✓
Eating a good meal, snack, or special treat	
Enjoying your favorite hot or cold beverage	
Cooking or baking, alone or with others	
Lying down, resting, or napping	
Exercising, stretching, doing yoga	
Receiving a massage, or massaging yourself	
Hugging or being close to someone physically	
Playing with children, or watching children play	
Talking with a good friend or loved one	
Engaging in sexual activity	
Playing a game with someone	
Spending time on social media	
Sitting or walking outside and viewing nature	
Looking at art	
Cuddling with a pet	
Reading a book, poetry, the newspaper, or an article	
Writing, journaling, or blogging	
Creating art, painting, doodling, drawing	
Listening to music or sounds of nature	
Singing, dancing, laughing, smiling	

Activities That Might Be Fun or Enjoyable	✓
Engaging in your religious or spiritual practice	
Complimenting or doing something nice for someone	
Taking care of a person or animal	
Watching your favorite movie or television show	

Identifying Mastery Activities

This set of activities is a bit different from the first. Unlike the pleasurable activities discussed above, mastery activities may not be fun or enjoyable in the moment. Although some may bring you enjoyment or pleasure, others may be stressful, challenging, or boring. However, we think of these as positive experiences because they can make you feel competent and capable, which can make you feel better about yourself and reduce your vulnerability to shame. Think about it: it will be much harder for shame to take hold of your life if you feel good about yourself and proud of your accomplishments. In fact, pride is considered the opposite of shame; it's hard to feel shame and pride at the same time. Therefore, one helpful way to reduce your vulnerability to shame is to do things every day that make you feel competent and capable.

As with the pleasurable activities we discussed earlier, the first step in incorporating mastery activities into your life is to identify the activities that bring you a sense of accomplishment and make you feel capable. Exercise 4.3 lists a number of different activities that may provide you with a sense of mastery or accomplishment. Although not all of these activities may work for you, this list will give you a sense of the types of activities that can make people feel competent and capable. As you review this list, consider if the activity stands out to you as something that may give you a sense of accomplishment or make you feel better about yourself. Place a check mark next to any you think might provide you with a sense of mastery. You might even find that this list sparks some new ideas for activities that you'd like to try. Once again, we've included some blank lines at the bottom of the table so that you can write in some of your own mastery activities.

Exercise 4.3: Identifying Possible Mastery Activities

Activities That Might Give You a Sense of Accomplishment or Mastery	✓
Spending time working on an important task	
Having a difficult conversation with someone	
Standing up for your feelings, wishes, or needs	
Going out when you don't feel like leaving your home	
Washing your car, or organizing and tidying a room	
Working on a puzzle or challenging game	
Socializing with others when you'd prefer to be alone	
Speaking or eating in front of others	
Doing something you've been avoiding	
Trying something new or a little scary	
Taking care of bills or finances	
Creating or organizing a to-do list	
Reading a challenging book	
Working on or completing a writing project	
Doing some research on jobs or volunteer work	
Doing volunteer work, helping others	
Cooking a new or challenging meal	
Solving a daily life problem of some kind	
Practicing music, martial arts, or another skill	
Learning a new computer application or operating system	

Activities That Might Give You a Sense of Accomplishment or Mastery	✓
Working on goals for personal growth or therapy	
Fixing or building something	
Doing laundry, vacuuming, or other housework	
Helping someone with homework or another difficult task	
Organizing an event, party, or celebration	
Teaching someone how to do something	
Working on health or financial goals	
Using new skills, such as the skills in this book	

Identifying Meaningful Activities That Matter to You

Another way to incorporate more positive experiences into your life is to do things that are important to you and bring your life meaning. Although some of these activities may overlap with those you identified previously, that won't always be the case. Unlike the pleasurable and mastery activities you identified, the activities we're talking about here may not be fun or enjoyable in the moment and may not give you an immediate sense of mastery or accomplishment. These activities could even be challenging or emotionally painful at times. Nonetheless, we think of these as positive experiences because they can bring about a greater sense of fulfillment and well-being and increase your overall sense of happiness. In fact, meaningful activities may be even more helpful than pleasurable and mastery activities in bringing about the long-lasting and sustainable positive emotions that can best reduce your vulnerability to emotions like shame.

Now, when it comes to identifying meaningful activities, it can be helpful to reflect on the things that matter to you. You can start by asking yourself the following questions:

What matters to me?

_____

_____

_____

What is important to me?

_____

_____

_____

What gives my life meaning?

_____

_____

_____

What makes me feel like I did something important or made a difference?

_____

_____

_____

What brings value to my life?

_____

_____

_____

What brings me a sense of fulfillment?

_____

_____

_____

Take some time to think about these questions and the answers that come to mind for you. Also, keep in mind that there are no right or wrong answers here. The only thing that matters is that you start the process of identifying the activities that bring your life meaning.

As another way of beginning to identify meaningful activities in life, exercise 4.4 lists a number of different overarching categories or types of activities that can bring meaning to a person's life. As with the other lists we provided above, this list is not exhaustive (the number of different types of activities that may be meaningful to someone is too large to count!) and not all types of activities on this list may be meaningful to you. The idea is not to force yourself to find meaning in these types of activities, but to give you a sense of the types of activities that some people find meaningful. So, after you've reflected on the questions above, review this list and see if any of these types of activities stand out to you. Then, for the ones you think may be meaningful to you, see if you can identify three to five specific activities that fall within that category that you could do in the next days or weeks. (You can download this exercise at http://www.newharbinger.com/49616.)

Exercise 4.4: Identifying Possible Meaningful Activities

Below is a list of different types of activities that might bring your life meaning or provide you with fulfillment. Place a check mark next to any that stand out to you. Then, for each type of activity you checked, try to identify three to five specific activities that would fall within this category that you could do in the coming days or weeks. Write those on the lines below each of the categories you marked.

Helping Others (people, animals, causes)	✓
Specific activity:	
Specific activity:	
Specific activity:	
Specific activity:	
Specific activity:	
Learning and Discovering New Things	✓
Specific activity:	
Specific activity:	
Specific activity:	
Specific activity:	
Specific activity:	
Contributing to the Community, Society, or the World	✓
Specific activity:	
Specific activity:	
Specific activity:	
Specific activity:	
Specific activity:	

Working Against Injustice, Inequality, Cruelty, Poverty, or Other Problems	✓
Specific activity:	
Specific activity:	
Specific activity:	
Specific activity:	
Specific activity:	
Being a Loving and Caring Family Member or Friend	✓
Specific activity:	
Specific activity:	
Specific activity:	
Specific activity:	
Specific activity:	
Caring for Others	✓
Specific activity:	
Specific activity:	
Specific activity:	
Specific activity:	
Specific activity:	
Caring for Your Body and Improving Your Physical Health	✓
Specific activity:	
Specific activity:	

Specific activity:	
Specific activity:	
Specific activity:	
Living an Active and Healthy Life	✓
Specific activity:	
Specific activity:	
Specific activity:	
Specific activity:	
Specific activity:	
Caring for the Environment or World	✓
Specific activity:	
Specific activity:	
Specific activity:	
Specific activity:	
Specific activity:	
Other Type of Activity:	✓
Specific activity:	
Specific activity:	
Specific activity:	
Specific activity:	
Specific activity:	

Other Type of Activity:	✓
Specific activity:	
Specific activity:	
Specific activity:	
Specific activity:	
Specific activity:	
Other Type of Activity:	✓
Specific activity:	
Specific activity:	
Specific activity:	
Specific activity:	
Specific activity:	

Incorporating Positive Activities into Your Life

Now that you've identified different activities that may bring you pleasure, mastery, or meaning, it's time to come up with a plan for incorporating these activities into your life. The more you can build these types of positive experiences into your daily life, the better you will feel. As we mentioned earlier, it's easier to manage negative emotions like shame if you experience positive emotions throughout your day as well. In addition, because some of these mastery and meaningful activities can make you feel better about yourself, they are particularly well suited for combating feelings of shame. Thus, incorporating these positive activities into your life will go a long way toward improving your mood and reducing your vulnerability to shame.

The next exercise can help you with this! Using the activities you identified so far, complete exercise 4.5 to make a plan to try at least two of these activities each day over the next week. As you plan for the week, make sure to include a combination of pleasurable, mastery, and meaningful activities. Incorporating each of these into your daily life will provide the best buffer against feelings of shame. It can also be helpful to try out different activities throughout the week so that you can figure out which work best for you. It's okay if some of the activities you identified don't end up working out as you hoped they would. For example, you may not enjoy some of the pleasurable activities as much as you thought you would, or you might not feel a sense of accomplishment from some of the mastery activities you try. That's okay. What matters is that you are giving yourself permission to have positive experiences and that you are working to identify the types of activities that will be the best fit for you. Like we said before, some of this is really about trial and error and just seeing what works. The key is to approach these activities with an open mind and commit to trying some each day.

Use this form to help track your experience of these activities and identify the ones that are most positive for you. (You can download this exercise at http://www.newharbinger.com/49616.)

Exercise 4.5: Incorporating Positive Activities into Your Daily Life

The goal of this exercise is to help you incorporate pleasurable, mastery, and meaningful activities into your daily life, and to track how positive each activity was for you. You will see that the types of positive emotions you are asked to track vary depending on the type of activity. For example, you'll be asked to monitor the pleasure or enjoyment you get from the pleasurable activities and the sense of mastery or accomplishment you get from the mastery activities.

In the first column, write down all of the different activities you plan to try this week. You can see that this column has three separate sections corresponding to the three different types of activities. Make sure to write down some activities in each of the sections so that you will have a mix of pleasurable, mastery, and meaningful activities in your week. In the second column, write the day you plan to do this activity. The goal is to try two different activities each day. It's okay if you want to try some activities on more than one day, although we recommend trying at least nine to ten different activities across the week. Then, in the third column, rate the positive emotions you experienced as a result of this activity, where 0 equals no positive emotions, 5 equals moderate positive emotions, and 10 equals the most intense positive emotions possible. After that, all that's left is to try out these activities and see which are a good fit for you!

Possible pleasurable activity	When do you plan to do this (that is, what day this week)?	Level of pleasure/ enjoyment you experienced (0–10)

Possible mastery activity	When do you plan to do this (that is, what day this week)?	Level of mastery/ accomplishment you experienced (0–10)

Possible meaningful activity	When do you plan to do this (that is, what day this week)?	Level of meaning/ fulfillment you experienced (0–10)

Connecting with These Positive Experiences and Their Associated Emotions

Now that you've identified activities that will bring you pleasure, mastery, and meaning and begun to incorporate these into your daily life, the final step is to engage in these activities in such a way that you can really connect to the experience. As you may have experienced in your own life, it's possible to engage in an activity without really connecting to or experiencing that activity. You can think of it as being on autopilot or just going through the motions. If you've had that experience, then you've probably noticed that you don't get as much from an experience if you aren't really present. The bottom line is that just doing these types of positive activities is not enough—you really need to connect with the experience and any positive emotions that come from it. In fact, making sure you engage in these activities mindfully is just as important as doing them at all. If you don't connect with the experience, you won't be able to get all of the benefits that go along with these activities.

To ensure that you're able to benefit the most from these activities, use the DBT mindfulness skill of throwing yourself completely into whatever you are doing in the moment (Linehan 1993b). The goal of this skill is to immerse yourself in your experiences, connecting with them completely. This skill will help you get the most out of what you're doing and fully connect with the positive experiences you're incorporating into your life. So, as you try out the different pleasurable, mastery, and meaningful activities you identified for the week, practice bringing your full attention and awareness to whatever activity you are doing at the time. Focus all of your attention on throwing yourself into this experience. If you get distracted by shame-related thoughts that you don't deserve positive experiences, simply notice these thoughts and then gently turn your attention back to the present moment and the activity at hand. Do this as many times as you need to, refocusing your attention again and again and again.

Finally, to help you connect with any positive emotions that come from these positive activities, use the DBT skill of mindfully noticing and attending to your emotions (Linehan 1993b). Positive emotions can provide a buffer against feelings of shame and give you more resources for combating those feelings. However, if you haven't had many positive experiences lately, or if your shame tells you that you are not deserving of these experiences, then it can be very challenging to connect with any positive emotions you do experience. To assist with this, it can be helpful to focus all of your attention on the emotions you are experiencing in the moment. Therefore, as you're engaging in the positive activities you identified earlier in this chapter, bring your attention to the emotions you're experiencing in the moment, noticing any sensations of emotions that may be present. Whatever you are feeling, simply pay attention to it and notice it. If your mind wanders or you get distracted, then gently guide your attention back to your emotions. Remind yourself that it's okay to feel whatever you are feeling. Give yourself permission to experience any positive emotions that may be present.

MOVING FORWARD

This chapter focused on skills you can use to reduce your vulnerability to intense shame. The less frequently you experience shame and the less intense it is when you do experience it, the easier it will be to manage it and lessen its hold on your life. Therefore, one of the first steps in learning how to manage your shame is to reduce your vulnerability for experiencing intense shame. You can do this by taking care of yourself physically and increasing the positive experiences in your life—both of which will help buffer against the experience of intense shame. And, remember, by taking care of yourself and treating yourself as if you are worthy and deserving of positive experiences in life, you will be combating shame directly by acting counter to the messages it sends that you are unworthy or undeserving. So, take this as an opportunity to give yourself permission to treat yourself with care, kindness, and compassion, and to begin to incorporate positive activities of all kinds into your life.

Although taking steps to combat intense shame before it arises by reducing your vulnerability for even experiencing intense shame is a great place to start, there will still be times when you experience shame. Therefore, it is important to have skills for managing shame when it occurs. The good news is that there are numerous DBT skills that are incredibly useful for managing shame and lessening its hold on your life. The next few chapters focus on these skills.

CHAPTER 5

Using Mindfulness Skills to Help Manage Shame

Chapter 4 provided you with some helpful skills for reducing your vulnerability to intense shame. Although these skills will go a long way toward helping you manage your shame, they are only one set of tools in your toolkit for building a life free from shame. This chapter provides you with another set of tools that will help you prevent shame from occurring and cope with it more effectively when it arises. The more tools you have at your disposal, the better equipped you'll be to change your patterns of shame and lessen the hold it has on your life.

This chapter focuses on how you can use DBT mindfulness skills to manage shame. As we discussed in chapter 2, there are several DBT mindfulness skills that can help you cope with feelings of shame. If you recall that mindfulness involves being more aware of your experiences (including your emotions), you might be wondering why you'd want to use these skills to help you manage shame. You might be asking yourself, *Why would I want to be mindful of my shame?* or *Why would I want to be more in touch with my shame when it's already so all-consuming?* Those are understandable questions. If you're like most people who struggle with intense shame, you probably feel as if you're already painfully aware of your shame much of the time. Therefore, it may seem odd to use skills focused on becoming more aware of your emotions to manage feelings of shame. You might be thinking that the best skills for shame would be the ones that allow you to distract yourself from feelings of shame. And distraction can definitely be helpful for shame. In fact, you will be learning about some of those skills in chapter 6. However, as surprising at it may sound, mindfulness skills can also be very helpful for recovering from shame.

There are a couple of reasons why this is the case. First, mindful awareness is quite different from the type of awareness that many people have of shame. Generally speaking, shame consumes people's attention in an all-encompassing and unhelpful way, pulling them in and keeping them stuck in the experience of the emotion. Mindfulness, on the other hand, can help you approach your emotions in a more helpful way, noticing and observing your emotions without getting caught up in them or consumed by them. In addition, mindfulness skills can actually help you take a step back from feelings of shame by focusing your attention on something else. In this way, these skills can help you distract yourself from feelings of shame at times.

SKILLS FOR REDUCING JUDGMENTS THAT LEAD TO SHAME

As we discussed in chapters 1 and 3, shame tends to be driven by negative self-judgments and evaluations. One of the main reasons people struggle with shame is that they judge themselves as bad, flawed, unworthy, or unacceptable. When those judgments arise, shame is the natural outcome. How would it be possible for someone to have those kinds of thoughts and judgments about themselves and not experience shame? For this reason, one of the best ways to combat shame and stop it in its tracks is to reduce self-judgments. If we could wave a magic wand and get rid of all of your negative judgments and evaluations of yourself, we could put an end to your struggles with shame. Unfortunately, we do not have such a magic wand (and believe us, we would use it if we had it!). What we can do, though, is teach you some DBT mindfulness skills that can help you reduce self-judgments and the feelings of shame that go along with them.

One way to prevent shame is to use the mindfulness skills of nonjudgmentally noticing and labeling your experience (Linehan 1993b, 2015) when you encounter one of your shame cues. Specifically, when you encounter something that tends to elicit shame for you (for example, if you make a mistake, do something that hurts someone else, or are judged by someone else for some aspect of your identity), refrain from judging yourself or using inflammatory language such as "evil" or "horrible" or "bad" to describe yourself or your behaviors. This will only intensify feelings of shame and make you feel worse. Instead, focus on simply describing what happened objectively, letting go of any evaluations or judgments (Linehan 1993b, 2015). For example, if you hurt your friend's feelings by forgetting their birthday, don't judge yourself as a horrible friend or your behavior of forgetting their birthday as selfish or rude. Instead, focus on objectively describing what happened by sticking to the facts. In this case, you might say, *I didn't remember it was my friend's birthday and so I forgot to call or text her "Happy Birthday." When I remembered three days later, I reached out to her and apologized. She told me that she appreciated my apology as her feelings had been hurt.* This is an example of sticking to the facts rather than adding on your evaluations or assessments of yourself or what you did (for example, by calling yourself a bad friend or judging your behavior as selfish). It takes the negative judgments out of the equation and leaves you with just the facts of what happened (which are far less likely to intensify shame). You'll get additional opportunities to practice this skill in chapter 7.

Now, you will probably notice that judgments and evaluations continue to pop into your head as you are using this skill, especially when you first start practicing it. This is completely natural. If this happens, simply notice those evaluations and judgments and then bring your attention back to noticing and describing your experience as objectively as possible. As we say in DBT, one of the most important things when you notice these judgments and evaluations is to not judge them! We don't want to inadvertently give you more things to judge about yourself. So, when you notice judgments arise, don't judge yourself for having those judgments. Instead, just notice them and turn your attention back to objectively noticing and labeling your experience.

In addition to combating self-judgments directly, noticing and describing your experience in a nonjudgmental and objective way will help you better understand what happened and figure out if there are more effective ways to handle the situation in the future. Although some people think that labeling experiences objectively without judgment will interfere with their ability to change things they don't like about themselves or their behaviors, this couldn't be further from the truth. In fact, it's only when you understand exactly what happened that you can figure out how to change the things you want to change. So, the next time you notice that you are judging yourself or your behaviors, focus on noticing and describing your experience in a nonjudgmental and objective way.

Maggie's Story

For as long as she could remember, Maggie had judged herself. She judged herself for almost everything: the things she did, who she was, and her sexual identity. She couldn't make it through a couple of hours, much less a day, without judging herself for something. Any time she wasn't perfect or let someone down in some way, she would beat herself up, calling herself a terrible person who wasn't worthy of anything positive in life.

When Maggie learned about the DBT mindfulness skill of nonjudgmentally noticing and labeling experiences, it resonated with her immediately. Although it seemed near impossible to imagine a life without almost constant self-judgments, she could see how this could be helpful. Therefore, she made a commitment to use this skill whenever she noticed she was judging herself, and it wasn't long before she had her chance.

Later that morning at work, her boss checked in with her about a report that had been due the night before. When she realized that she'd forgotten to complete it, Maggie noticed that she started beating herself up, calling herself stupid and lazy and incompetent. As soon as she noticed these judgments, she reminded herself to practice the skill of nonjudgmentally describing her experiences.

She took a breath and described what had happened objectively, saying to herself, My report was due last night and I forgot to submit it. My boss checked in about the status of the report today and reminded me it was overdue. She asked me to submit it by the end of the day. She said that as long as she could review it first thing in the morning, she'd have plenty of time. I will submit it before I leave work today. As soon as Maggie described what happened in this way, she noticed that her shame became less intense and she was able to take a step back from those feelings and focus on getting her report done.

Although this experience reinforced her commitment to use this skill whenever she noticed self-judgments, as the afternoon went on, she also noticed that this was easier said than done, as the same self-judgments kept popping into her mind while she worked on the report. However, she remembered the DBT saying to not judge your judgments, and so she just kept turning her attention back to describing her experience and behavior nonjudgmentally.

After a few days of trying this skill, she noticed that it was getting a bit easier to do and she was better able to take a step back from her judgments when she noticed them. And, a few days after that, she noticed that her self-judgments had lessened and she wasn't beating herself up as much anymore.

SKILLS FOR NOT GETTING CAUGHT UP IN SHAME-RELATED THOUGHTS

It can be very easy to get caught up in the thoughts that go along with shame. In fact, this is one of the things that makes shame so challenging to manage. The thoughts that go along with shame tend to grab people's attention and not let go. Rather than passing through your mind easily, these thoughts are "sticky." It can be really difficult to take a step back from them. And this makes a lot of sense when you think about the types of thoughts that go along with shame. As we've discussed before, these thoughts tend to be fairly extreme and powerful judgments that are difficult to let go. If you think that you're a terrible person, or worthless, or undeserving of anything positive in life, it makes sense that it would be difficult to detach yourself from these thoughts. They grab your attention. That's where DBT mindfulness skills come into play.

Notice Shame-Related Thoughts Without Attaching to Them

One of the most useful skills for dealing with sticky shame-related thoughts is the DBT mindfulness skill of noticing thoughts without attaching to, reacting to, or acting on these thoughts (Linehan

1993b). In the *Skills Training Manual for Treating Borderline Personality Disorder* (Linehan 1993b), this specific skill is described as having a "Teflon mind." Basically, the idea is to allow thoughts to slide out of your mind in the same way that the nonstick Teflon coating on pans allows food to slide out of the pan when you're cooking. If you've ever tried cooking something like a fried egg, omelet, or grilled cheese sandwich in a pan without a Teflon coating (or something similar), then you've probably noticed that food tends to stick to the bottom of the pan when it doesn't have this coating, making it hard to remove the food from the pan.

So, what does this have to do with managing shame-related thoughts? Well, the same principles apply to thoughts that go through our minds. If you don't practice having a "Teflon mind," shame-related thoughts will be much more likely to stick in your mind rather than sliding out easily like other thoughts that aren't distressing tend to do. So, the goal of this mindfulness skill is to allow your shame-related thoughts to pass in and out of your mind without getting stuck to them. Use exercise 5.1 to help you practice this skill and take a step back from shame-related thoughts. To listen to recorded instructions, visit http://www.newharbinger.com/49616.

Exercise 5.1: Practicing Teflon Mind

1. Find a comfortable and quiet place where you can sit or lie down.

2. Close your eyes.

3. Take a few minutes to focus on your breath. Notice what it feels like to breathe in and breathe out. Notice what parts of your body move as you breathe in and out.

4. Picture your mind as a Teflon-coated pan that allows thoughts to slide in and out of your mind without getting stuck. Picture your mind as the pan and your thoughts as the food being cooked in the pan.

5. Take a few minutes to watch your thoughts sliding in and out of your mind, just as food slides out of a Teflon-coated pan. You don't need to generate any particular thoughts. Just notice any thoughts you are having and watch as they slide out of your mind.

6. If you find your thoughts getting stuck in your mind, notice that and then bring your attention back to allowing the thoughts to slide in and out of your mind.

Once you've practiced this exercise a few times, use it the next time you notice yourself getting caught up in shame-related thoughts. Just as you noticed other thoughts sliding in and out of your mind, picture your shame-related thoughts sliding in and out of your mind without getting stuck.

Another way to practice this skill is to picture placing each of the thoughts that go through your mind when you're experiencing shame on a conveyor belt (adapted from the *Skills Training Manual for Treating Borderline Personality Disorder*; Linehan 1993b). Conveyor belts tend to operate at a steady speed, moving objects slowly across a room. In the same way, you can picture all of your thoughts moving slowly and steadily across your mind. Don't try to change the speed of the conveyor belt, or take thoughts off the conveyor belt. Just notice each thought passing through your mind, one after another. If you notice that the conveyor belt stalls, or the thoughts start piling up on one another on the belt, or the thoughts start falling off the belt, just notice that experience and gently turn your attention back to the conveyor belt, placing each thought on the belt and noticing as it moves through your mind. The next time you experience shame, try to practice this exercise for at least five minutes. The more you practice it, the easier it will become to use this skill to manage shame-related thoughts.

Label Shame-Related Thoughts as Thoughts

Another skill that can be helpful in dealing with shame-related thoughts is the DBT mindfulness skill of labeling your experience (Linehan 1993b). One of the reasons people tend to get so attached to and caught up in shame-related thoughts is that they buy into these thoughts as literally true. Rather than recognizing negative self-judgments as simply thoughts generated by their mind that may not be true or accurate, people who struggle with shame tend to buy into these negative evaluations of themselves as truth. That's why this skill can be so helpful. Labeling a thought as just a thought is one way to keep yourself from buying into your thoughts or responding as if they were true. This skill will help you recognize that shame-related thoughts are simply thoughts generated by your mind rather than an accurate and objective description of how things are.

So, the next time you have a shame-related thought or self-judgment, make sure to label that as just a thought. For example, rather than thinking to yourself *I am a horrible person*, or *I am worthless*, make sure to describe these thoughts as just thoughts by saying something like *I am having the thought that I am a horrible person*, or *I am having the thought that I am worthless*. Approaching shame-related thoughts in this way and clearly labeling them as they are—just thoughts your mind has generated—will help you take a step back from these thoughts and not buy into them as if they were literally true. To help you with this, write down your shame-related thoughts on the worksheet for exercise 5.2. (If you prefer, you can download this exercise at http://www.newharbinger.com/49616.)

Exercise 5.2: Labeling Your Shame-Related Thoughts as Just Thoughts

Use this worksheet to help you connect with the fact that your negative self-judgments and other shame-related thoughts are just thoughts. Write down all of your typical shame-related thoughts below.

I am having the thought that _____

_____

I am having the thought that _____

_____

I am having the thought that _____

_____

I am having the thought that _____

_____

I am having the thought that _____

_____

I am having the thought that _____

_____

I am having the thought that _____

_____

I am having the thought that _____

_____

SKILLS FOR FOCUSING YOUR ATTENTION ON SOMETHING OTHER THAN SHAME

One reason that shame is such a painful and overwhelming emotion is that it is all-consuming. As we discussed earlier, shame tends to capture all of a person's attention when it's present. When you're experiencing shame, it can be hard to focus on anything else. This is why shame can so easily spiral out of control. Basically, you can get sucked into a vicious cycle of experiencing shame, attaching or buying into shame-related negative evaluations, experiencing more shame, and so on. To break this cycle and give you the space to be able to use other skills, it can be helpful to give yourself a break from shame by focusing your attention on something else.

Now, you might be thinking to yourself that this sounds easier said than done. If shame is so powerful and attention-grabbing, how could you focus on anything else? Well, that's where DBT mindfulness skills come into play again. Basically, because these skills are all about directing our attention and awareness in ways that are most effective, you can use these skills to focus on something other than shame.

Notice and Label the Information Coming Through Your Senses

One of the simplest ways to help you focus your attention on something other than shame is to use the DBT skills of noticing and labeling your experience (Linehan 1993b) to focus your attention on your five senses. You can think of this as a first step in redirecting your attention. Basically, rather than directing your attention to shame-related cues, thoughts, and physical sensations, focus all of your attention on the information coming through each of your five senses: taste, touch, smell, sound, and sight. See if you can focus all of your attention on one sense at a time. Remember not to judge these experiences as good or bad, but just to focus on your senses and everything you're experiencing in the moment. Next, see if you can begin to label these experiences, putting words on your experiences and describing them in as much detail as possible. You can think of this as painting a picture of your experience with your words. To help you use this skill, ask yourself the questions in exercise 5.3.

Exercise 5.3: Questions to Help You Notice and Label the Information Coming Through Your Senses

Ask yourself these questions to help you get in touch with and describe the information coming through each of your five senses.

Taste

What do I taste right now?

Where do I first notice this taste in my mouth?

Is it subtle or strong?

Is it bitter, or sweet, or salty?

Is it cold or hot?

How long does the taste last?

Touch

What do I feel against my skin?

What do I feel against my fingertips?

What textures do I feel?

Is what I am feeling soft or hard?

Is it rough or smooth?

Is it warm or cool to the touch?

Smell

What scents do I notice?

Are they strong or mild?

How does the scent change over time?

How long does the scent last?

Sound

What am I hearing right now?

Are the sounds nearby or far away?

Are they loud or soft?

Is their pitch high or low?

How long does each sound last?

Sight

What do I see right now?

What objects do I observe?

What color(s) do I notice?

What textures and patterns do I see?

What shapes do I see?

Focusing on your five senses will help redirect your attention to something other than your feelings of shame. Try this the next time you find yourself being consumed by feelings of shame and see how helpful it can be.

Notice and Label Your Entire Experience in the Moment

Another way to redirect your attention to something other than shame is to use the DBT skills of noticing and labeling your experience (Linehan 1993b) to help you get in touch with everything you're experiencing in the moment. Even though it can be difficult to connect with any other aspect of your experience when shame is present, that doesn't mean that those other aspects aren't present too. Even when people are experiencing intense shame, it's common for other emotions and thoughts to be present as well. It's just harder to recognize these when shame is intense. Therefore, noticing and labeling all aspects of your experience can help you expand your attention to other thoughts and feelings beyond shame.

Now, you may be wondering why we separated this skill from the skill of noticing and labeling sensory information, or why we discussed that skill first. Well, we think of the previous skill as an excellent first step for practicing these mindfulness skills. When people are just beginning to use these skills, it can be helpful to have something specific, simple, and concrete to focus all of their attention on—something that is always present no matter what. Therefore, starting by focusing on your five senses is a great first step. However, it is also important to be able to expand your awareness to other internal experiences you're having beyond shame, like your other emotions and thoughts. That way, you will have a more complete understanding of your full experience in the moment. So, that's why we recommend using these skills to help you get in touch with all aspects of your experience in the moment (rather than just the information coming in through your five senses). Ask yourself the questions in exercise 5.4 to help you fully connect with all aspects of your experience in the present moment.

Exercise 5.4: Questions to Help You Connect with the Present Moment

Ask yourself these questions to help you get in touch with everything you are experiencing in the present moment.

Present External Environment

What do I see right now?

What objects do I observe?

Are there other people around? If so, what do they look like? What are they doing? What facial expressions do they have?

What do I feel against my skin?

What do I feel against my fingertips?

What am I hearing right now?

Are the sounds nearby or far away?

_____

_____

_____

_____

Present Internal Environment

How do I feel right now?

What emotions am I having other than shame?

What thoughts are running through my mind right now?

How does my body feel?

Am I cold, or hot, or warm?

Are my muscles relaxed or tense?

Where do I notice tension in my body right now?

_____

_____

_____

_____

As you start practicing this exercise, you might notice that it can be very difficult to expand your attention beyond your feelings of shame, and that's okay. In fact, that's to be expected. If this was easy to do, we wouldn't have an entire book focused on helping people manage their shame. The good news, though, is that just practicing this skill—even if it doesn't go as smoothly as you'd like—will be helpful in and of itself. Like so many of the skills we review in this book, mindfulness skills become easier to use over time. The more you practice expanding your awareness to other emotions, thoughts, and physical sensations you're experiencing in addition to shame, the more you'll get used to doing this and the easier it will become.

Focus Your Attention on One Thing at a Time

The DBT skill of focusing attention on one thing at a time (Linehan 1993b) is another skill that can help you focus your attention on something other than shame. Specifically, the idea behind this skill is to focus all of your attention on whatever you are doing in that moment, gently guiding your attention back to the present moment and the task at hand whenever you are distracted by feelings of shame. So, using this skill will help you redirect your attention to whatever it is you are doing in the moment—anything at all. The only thing that matters is that you continue to return your attention to the task at hand when you feel yourself distracted by shame. So, if you are working, work. If you are exercising, exercise. If you are writing, write. If you are playing with your children, play with your children. If you are doing something comforting or self-soothing, focus all of your attention on just that. This will give you something else to focus on other than shame and will also help you connect with the positive or meaningful aspects of these other activities.

So, the next time you find yourself getting caught up in feelings of shame or shame-related thoughts, take a deep breath and then bring your attention back to whatever you were doing in that moment. Focus all of your attention on just that one thing, throwing yourself into that activity and concentrating your mind only on that. If you get distracted by your shame, notice that and then bring your attention back to the activity at hand. Do this as many times as you need to, refocusing your attention again and again and again.

Steve's Story

When Steve learned about using DBT mindfulness skills to help him manage feelings of shame, he was skeptical to say the least. He felt as if he couldn't get away from his feelings of shame, as his negative self-judgments, sinking feeling and pit in his stomach, and urges to hide and beat himself up were almost always present. The idea that being more mindful and aware of these feelings would be helpful just didn't make a lot of sense to him.

However, Steve was committed to doing everything he could to overcome his feelings of shame and build a life free from their hold on him. Therefore, he decided to try these skills and see if they would help. Initially, he chose to practice using the DBT mindfulness skills to focus his attention on something other than shame. Focusing on his five senses seemed like a great place to start, so he began to do that whenever he found himself getting caught up in feelings of shame. He even started carrying around some things he could use to make that exercise easier and more enjoyable, like his favorite hard candies and pictures of vacation spots he found relaxing.

Once he felt like he had a good sense of how that mindfulness skill worked, he tried focusing his attention on the other thoughts and feelings he was having in addition to shame. Sure enough, he soon realized that even though it seemed like shame was the only feeling present, there were often other emotions and thoughts present too, from feelings of love and happiness when he spent time with his partner or children to feelings of excitement and even pride at work. Focusing on those helped give him a break from the shame.

In the end, though, the skill he found most helpful was to focus all of his attention on what he was doing in the moment. When he was at work, he focused all of his attention on teaching the students in his class. When he noticed self-judgments pop up, he simply turned his attention back to his students and what it was like to interact with them, focusing on the things they were saying and the information he was trying to get across. When he was with his partner and children, he focused all of his attention on being with them and the conversations they were having, noticing everything about the experience of just being with these people he cared about.

After practicing that skill for a week, he realized how often he hadn't really been present in his life and how much his shame had distracted him from the things that mattered to him in his life, like spending time with his family and teaching the students in his class. By focusing his attention completely on those activities, he found that not only did he get some relief from his shame, he also felt more connected to the people and experiences in his life that he cared about.

MOVING FORWARD

This chapter focused on how to use DBT mindfulness skills to prevent and manage shame. You learned skills to stop shame from arising by describing yourself and your behaviors in an objective and nonjudgmental way rather than falling into a pattern of negative self-judgments and evaluations. You also learned skills for coping with shame when it does arise by taking a step back from shame-related thoughts and not getting caught up in these thoughts. Finally, you learned skills for redirecting your attention to thoughts, feelings, and experiences other than shame in order to give yourself a break from feelings of shame and connect with other aspects of your experience.

Together, these skills can be incredibly helpful for changing how you respond to both shame cues and experiences of shame that arise, and they will go a long way in limiting the power shame has over your life. As you practice these skills, though, remember that changing how you respond to shame and shame cues is a process that takes time. These patterns aren't going to change overnight. Therefore, the important thing is just to keep practicing these mindfulness skills when you notice shame and shame-related thoughts, and refrain from judging yourself if you get distracted by shame or if self-judgments arise. The more you use these skills, the more natural it will feel to approach yourself and your experiences with nonjudgmental awareness.

Now that you've learned a number of different mindfulness skills for preventing and coping with shame, the next chapter focuses on distress tolerance skills you can use to avoid making things worse when you're experiencing shame.

CHAPTER 6

How to Avoid Making Things Worse When You Feel Shame

Shame can be a very painful emotion—one you'd probably rather avoid if you could. Indeed, intense shame is one of the most difficult feelings to tolerate. When intense shame arises, the desire to get away from it can be incredibly strong. When it arises, the urge to escape it can be difficult to resist and lead to all kinds of harmful behaviors to avoid it, such as using substances or self-harming. You might also do or say things to other people that you later regret. In this chapter, we discuss some key DBT skills to help you avoid doing things that can make an already painful situation worse.

We focus in this chapter on a couple of the DBT distress tolerance skills that we think will help most with shame. One of these skills includes the crisis survival skill of distraction, and the other one includes radical acceptance.

CRISIS SURVIVAL SKILLS AND DISTRACTION

The primary goal of crisis survival skills is to help you avoid making a difficult situation worse than it already is—basically, to "survive" the crisis you're in without making things more stressful for yourself. These skills will help you ride out a difficult situation without acting on your emotions or urges. They might also help take the edge off intense emotions like shame, making them a little more bearable. We're going to focus here primarily on the crisis survival skill of distraction.

Distraction is one of the DBT distress tolerance crisis survival skills. *Distraction* involves focusing your attention on something other than your emotional pain or stress. When you attend to something else, you'll probably find that you get a short reprieve from emotional pain (including shame). You might also be less likely to act on your shame in a way that makes things worse. You can distract yourself in many ways, and in this chapter, we describe a couple of ways to do this.

Distracting Yourself by Engaging in Activities

Distraction by engaging in activities involves doing things that are interesting enough to draw your mind away from your emotional pain. If you're feeling intense shame and having a hard time tolerating it, distracting yourself by doing some kind of engaging and interesting activity may help. The best activities are interesting, compelling, and stimulating. If you choose a boring or uninteresting activity, it won't capture your attention and you'll probably find that your mind wanders back to the source of your shame. If you choose something interesting or compelling, you'll have an easier time remaining focused and get more of a break from shame.

Which distracting activities you choose will probably depend on the situation you're in. You might do different things to distract yourself if you're alone versus with other people. Here are some things you can do to distract yourself if you're alone:

- Leave your home and go for a stimulating walk, run, or hike.

- Contact a support person and arrange to get together.

- Go outside and watch birds or other wildlife.

- Go for a walk in a natural setting.

- Go someplace where there are a lot of people doing interesting things—for example, a fair, park, coffee shop, restaurant, or library.

- Go swimming, work out, or sit in a hot tub or sauna.

- Play, compose, or listen to music.

- Cook or bake.

- Watch your favorite television show, movie, or sporting event.

- Go to a sporting event at a local stadium.

- Go to your favorite restaurant.

- Dance or sing.

When you're alone, it can also be helpful to get a change of scenery. Let's say you're feeling intense shame and you're alone in your home, sitting on the couch or something. Well, it can be helpful to get out of the place where you're feeling shame. Marsha Linehan sometimes used to tell clients to not "hang out at the cemetery." Try to use activities that get you out and about in a different environment.

If you're feeling a lot of shame while you're with other people, you might use different distraction strategies. Let's say you're out with a group of people, and you notice strong shame arising. The shame makes you feel like avoiding people or leaving, when in your "wise mind" you know it would be best for you to stay. These are good friends or loved ones, and you value your time together, even though it can be hard. How do you distract yourself then? Here are some possibilities:

- Mindfully participate in the conversations you're having. Really focus mindfully on the person or people you're spending time with. Temporarily turn your attention away from your shame and toward the people around you. If you have shame-related thoughts (such as judgments about yourself or your appearance), turn your attention away from those too. This is the skill of mindfulness of others, and we'll revisit it in chapter 9.

- Take a little breather so that you can do something distracting alone, and then come back to the person or people you're with. You might, for example, go outside, walk around the block, listen to some music, or call someone you can talk to about how you're feeling.

- If you're out and a meal or activities, such as a game, are happening, focus on eating the meal or playing the game. Try to fill your whole mind with whatever activity you're doing so there's not much room left for shame and shame-related thoughts.

- Talk with one of the people you're with about how you're feeling and let them know you need some help getting your mind on something else.

Distracting Yourself by Getting Your Mind Busy

Doing something that gets your mind busy can take your attention away from your shame. If your mind is so busy with work, a difficult problem you're trying to solve, a puzzle, game, or other engaging activity, it will be easier to not focus on shame-related experiences.

- Do a Sudoku or crossword puzzle, Wordle, or some other puzzle/game that requires some effort.

- Play a game with someone else, ideally something that's a little difficult and keeps your attention focused. One game that can be useful to consider is Bananagrams. When you're playing this game, you're continually making words out of little tiles. Because you're trying to be the first to finish, you have to be quick. There's very little downtime, so there's also very little time to dwell on shame or shame-related experiences.

- Work on learning something new, such as a new language, or how to do math problems, a new and challenging video game, or a computer application.

- Engage in a physical activity that involves learning something new or improving something, such as practicing martial arts, working on your tennis swing, shooting basketball hoops, throwing darts, playing billiards or pool, or other similar activities.

- Choose a number divisible by 7, such as 210, and count backward until you reach 0 or, if you make a mistake, as close to 0 as possible. If you try this, you might have to let go of any judgments or shame about your arithmetic abilities!

Distracting Yourself with Strong Sensations

Another helpful way to distract yourself is to experience strong sensations that grab your attention. Loud and stimulating music, for example, can draw your attention away from strong emotions like shame. A deep-tissue massage might be so stimulating and relaxing that there's little room left to dwell on shame-related experiences and thoughts. Consider your five senses, including vision, taste, touch, smell, and hearing. Think about what you could do to experience strong sensations that temporarily get your mind off shame-related experiences and thoughts. Here are a few suggestions:

- **Vision.** Watch a beautiful sunset or sunrise; look at brightly colored flowers; watch interesting nature scenes or animals in the wild; watch engaging or interesting television or videos.

- **Taste.** Suck on a sour candy; bite into a slice of lemon or lime; eat spicy or heavily flavored food; chew strongly flavored gum (such as mint, sour, or cinnamon gum); eat your favorite meal or a delectable dessert.

- **Touch**. Give yourself a massage or get one from someone else; pet your cat or dog; rub your hand on a rough (or smooth) surface; squeeze a stress ball or play with Silly Putty; make a snowball with your bare hands; hold ice in a freezer bag (but not to the point of experiencing pain); wrap your hands around a warm cup of tea or coffee (but not hot enough to cause pain); cuddle or engage in sexual activity with someone.

- **Smell**. Smell something strongly scented, such as flowers, aromatherapy candles or oil, freshly baked goods, perfume or cologne, coffee or coffee beans, loose tea leaves, vinegar, or acidic fruit like a lemon or lime.

- **Hearing**. Listen to loud and stimulating music; go someplace where a lot of people are making a lot of noise (playground, sporting event, concert, or similar places); listen to different sounds from a sound machine or sound app on your phone; rub rough things together like sandpaper and listen to the sound they make; listen to audio clips or videos of interesting sounds that capture your attention, such as nature sounds, the sound of a busy market in a crowded city, and so forth.

Distracting Yourself by "Contributing"

Contributing is a skill in DBT that involves helping someone or something else. Focusing on the needs of someone else can be a great way to get your mind off shame and related experiences. When you're taking care of a pet, for example, you're probably mostly focused on what the pet needs rather than on how you're feeling or thinking about yourself. Similarly, when you engage in volunteer work, help others with a task, and so forth, you might get a temporary reprieve from shame. Moreover, helping others can help you feel better about yourself. Below are some suggestions for how you can use the skill of contributing to distract yourself from shame-related experiences. We've split these up into easier, little everyday things you can do and bigger things you can do that involve more work.

Little Everyday Things You Can Do to Contribute

- Help someone with a task, such as understanding their smartphone, lifting something, moving, mowing their lawn, or shoveling their driveway.

- Give someone a ride somewhere.

- Open the door for someone.

- Offer to edit someone's written work (such as an essay, homework, or job application).

- Make someone a meal.

- Visit someone who is alone or having a hard time.

- Call someone just to talk and offer support.

Bigger Things You Can Do to Contribute

- Engage in volunteer work.

- Assist with a campaign of some kind.

- Contribute work, time, or money to a cause that's important to you.

- Develop a new idea or initiative at work that will help others.

- Write a blog about your own experience with the goal of helping others.

- Seek a job where you can engage in activities that you value or that involve helping others.

Now, when you do these activities, it's important that you throw yourself into them and focus all of your attention on them. Immersing yourself fully in the experience is one of the mindfulness skills we taught you about in chapter 5. As we discussed in that chapter, it's important to throw your whole mind into your activity. Let's say you were to go for a walk in the woods, but instead of paying attention to the interesting scenery and wildlife, you spent the whole time thinking about what's upsetting you. How do you think you'd feel during that walk? Probably just as miserable as you were before you went on the walk! The goal of distraction is to throw yourself into your distracting activities to get a break from your shame and whatever caused it to arise. So, make sure you really focus your attention on the activity you're doing and your experience in the moment.

Exercise 6.1 will help you come up with a plan to replace actions that make things worse with distracting activities. Use this exercise to think of a situation in which you've felt shame, actions that made your situation worse, and how you can replace those actions in the future with distracting activities.

Exercise 6.1: Coming Up with a Distraction Plan

Describe a common situation in which you feel intense shame that is moderately difficult to tolerate. Make note of the kinds of things you've done in the past to try to escape those feelings of shame that may have made things worse. Then, write down distracting activities that you could do instead. Try to think of activities that are easy to do but interesting enough to get your mind off your shame. You're going to replace the possible "behaviors that make things worse" with distracting activities. Take a snapshot, scan, or make a copy of this form so you have your distraction plan available when you need it. (If you prefer, you can download this form at http://www.newharbinger.com/49616.)

Common situation in which I feel intense shame:

_____

_____

_____

_____

_____

Things I've sometimes done to escape shame that have made things worse for me:

_____

_____

_____

_____

_____

Distracting activities I could do instead:

_____

_____

_____

_____

_____

_____

_____

THE REALITY ACCEPTANCE SKILL OF RADICAL ACCEPTANCE

Like the crisis survival skills (and distraction in particular), the reality acceptance skills can help you avoid making things worse, but in a different way. The idea behind the reality acceptance skills is that emotional and physical pain is a normal part of life and, for the most part, not optional. Although there are skills that can lessen the intensity and frequency of shame, it isn't possible to avoid shame or the situations that prompt it altogether. Experiencing shame is a part of being human.

There are, however, things you can do to reduce how much you suffer when you feel shame. From a DBT perspective, suffering comes about when you refuse to accept pain. If you were to refuse to accept that you were experiencing shame, deny those feelings, judge yourself for feeling shame, or get caught up in bitterness and resentment toward other people for "making" you feel shame, you'd probably suffer a lot. Instead, consider what would happen if you were to acknowledge and accept that you feel shame. It would still be painful, but you'd be in a much better position to do something about it. Accepting the situation you're in and the experience of shame, at least for now, would help point you in the direction of the many skills in this book that you can use to manage shame. In turn, you'd probably suffer a lot less. That's what reality acceptance skills can help you do. We'll focus on one of these skills in particular: the skill of *radical acceptance.*

Let's say you unintentionally said something mean to your partner or friend. You were upset and frustrated, and the words just came out of your mouth. Immediately, you regretted what you said, and then you started to feel shame creeping in. You had thoughts that you're a "bad friend," a "mean person," that you can't control yourself and always "mess up" like this, and that your friend probably doesn't like you or want to be around you anymore. You feel a sinking sensation in the pit of your stomach, your face feels flushed, your muscles are tense, and you just want to leave and hide out in your bedroom.

Having already said something you regret, how can you avoid suffering more than you really have to? Well, one way to do that is to step back in your mind and acknowledge the situation for what it is. That's what radical acceptance is all about. You might say to yourself, *It's true, I said something I really didn't mean to say. I feel shame, and I regret saying it. The shame feels really painful right now, and I wish I could do something about it.* Instead of denying your feelings, the idea is to acknowledge and accept them. Then, you can figure out what to do about the situation, such as calling your friend, making amends, finding common ground, or using some of the DBT skills we've reviewed in this book. If, instead, you were to get swallowed up in shame, judge and criticize yourself, avoid or deny your feelings, and so forth, you'd probably end up suffering more—and you might not even take steps to fix the situation.

When people first hear the term "radical acceptance," they often question how this could be helpful. The reason we usually get these questions is because of the word "acceptance." If you're not familiar with DBT, referring to acceptance can make you think that we're suggesting that you need to like or be okay with difficult or painful situations, mistreatment by others, or feelings of shame. The good news is that this is *not* what we're suggesting at all or what the term acceptance refers to in DBT.

In DBT, acceptance does not mean that you have to like or approve of the pain you're experiencing. So, you can accept that you are experiencing shame and you can accept the situation or experience that led to feelings of shame without approving of those feelings or what happened. If someone judged you for some aspect of your identity, or told you that something about yourself was not okay, radically accepting the situation doesn't mean that you have to think what they did was okay. Instead, radical acceptance involves acknowledging that it happened, that you feel the way you do, and that things are difficult and painful. Accepting and acknowledging to yourself that you feel shame does not mean you agree that you should feel shame, or that you agree with the negative judgments about yourself that often accompany shame.

Practicing Radical Acceptance

Given how painful and difficult shame is, you might be wondering how on earth to practice the skill of radical acceptance. Fortunately, there are several ways to practice this skill. Here are a few of our favorites:

State what you're trying to accept out loud in a neutral or soft voice. Just state it without any judgments, describing the facts. Following from the previous example of saying something you regret to a friend, you might say, "I said things to Sandy that I really regret. The things I said were judgmental, and I didn't mean them. I wish I could take them back, but I can't. I feel shame and the urge to just hole up and be alone. I feel like never talking with Sandy again because it's too embarrassing to reach out now."

Write out what you want to work on accepting. As with the above practice (stating it out loud), write down what you want to accept, sticking to the facts, including the situation, your thoughts, and how you feel. Try this now. Write out the details of a situation that is bringing up shame for you, describing the situation and your experience of shame.

_____

_____

_____

_____

_____

_____

_____

Imagine what would be different if you were to accept things as they are. If you're having a hard time accepting something, that's okay. You don't have to accept it right now if you don't think you're ready. But you could imagine how things might be different if you were to accept it. For example, if you said something you regret to·a friend, you might imagine what you'd do if you accepted what you did and how you feel about it. Perhaps you'd imagine practicing radical acceptance for a little while, then picking up the phone and having a heart-to-heart talk with your friend. You might even imagine being open about how you feel about what you said, why you said it, and listening to how your friend feels about it. Imagine resolving things with your friend. Think of your own situation, and imagine what might be different if you were to accept the situation and any shame that seems to be coming up for you. Describe below what you imagined.

_____

_____

_____

_____

_____

_____

Assume an accepting body position while thinking of the thing you're having a hard time accepting. An accepting posture in DBT can involve the strategy of sitting (or standing) with an open posture. Sit in a relaxed position with your hands on your lap or the arms of a chair and your palms facing upward. Through your posture, you're sending the message to your brain that things will be okay. When you do this, try to relax the muscles in your body, face, and neck. If you want to amp up the effectiveness of this strategy, try putting a small half-smile on your face.

Half-smiling is another DBT skill, and it communicates to your brain that you're safe and things are going to be okay. Don't make it a big grin or artificial smile; a half-smile is like the smile you see in the *Mona Lisa* painting. Just gently turn up the corners of your mouth. Then, bring to mind the thing you're having a hard time accepting. Allow thoughts and images of the situation to come to mind. Allow yourself to feel whatever emotions come up and to experience whatever thoughts cross your mind.

Tips on Radical Acceptance

We have a few tips for you to consider regarding radical acceptance. One tip is that it's best to use this skill for situations or experiences that have happened in the past or that are happening right now. You can't radically accept something that hasn't yet occurred, so trying to accept the future won't work!

A second important tip about radical acceptance is to treat it as a practice. It's not as if you can just convince yourself to accept something, and then you're done. Radical acceptance is an ongoing practice; you have to keep doing it. It's a lot like staying fit. You can't just work out one day and become fit enough to run a marathon or enter a weightlifting competition. You have to work out steadily over time. Sometimes you'll see results. Sometimes there will be setbacks. Radical acceptance is similar. Sometimes you might find that you've come to terms with things that are hard to accept; other times, you'll find that things are harder. We're confident that if you keep practicing, you'll notice that your suffering and shame will diminish.

Self-Acceptance and Compassion for Yourself

Another way to practice radical acceptance is to turn the skill of acceptance toward yourself. Shame is one of those emotions that makes it hard to accept yourself. If you're feeling shame about who you are, you're probably not accepting yourself. Instead, you're probably thinking you shouldn't be the way you are. Practicing radical acceptance of yourself, therefore, can help you chip away at shame.

You can't really just tell yourself to accept yourself. It doesn't work that way. Instead, the best way to practice self-acceptance is to act as if you accept yourself, and act as if you have compassion toward yourself. Here are some ways to do that:

Take your feelings, thoughts, and opinions seriously. Act as if what you think and how you feel matter. Tell yourself it's understandable that you think and feel this way. Let's say a coworker criticizes you in a work meeting in front of a bunch of people. You feel hurt, ashamed, and embarrassed. You also think that this behavior was disrespectful and uncalled for. Using the skills we describe in chapter 9 for how to deal with shame in relationships, you decide to take your needs and opinions seriously. You ask your coworker to go for coffee so you can chat about what they said and how you felt.

Be open with yourself. If you're judging or feeling shame about some aspect of yourself, avoid hiding from yourself. If you feel shame about your body, look at it with openness, curiosity, and compassion. If you feel shame about your gender identity, engage in identity-affirming actions. Use pronouns you feel comfortable with, express those to others, and tell yourself that your identity is the way it is and there's nothing wrong with it.

Encourage yourself. One way to be kind to yourself is to be encouraging and positive toward yourself. Shame might make you feel like discouraging or disparaging yourself. You might have thoughts that you can't cope or you can't do things. Forget that! Instead, say things to yourself that are encouraging. Find a way to say to yourself, *I can do this. I can solve this problem* [whatever it might be], *cope with difficult things, handle painful emotions, and be skillful.* One way to practice this skill is to think of very stressful times in the past that you've managed to get through okay. If you can think of something that was even more stressful than what you're experiencing now, you could tell yourself, *I got through that, so I can get through this.*

Be welcoming toward yourself. Welcoming is kind of the opposite of rejecting. Shame makes you feel like rejecting yourself, so instead welcome yourself. One way to do this is to imagine that you open the door to your home. It's rainy and cold outside, and when you open the door, you see yourself standing there. Welcome yourself in from the rain. Open the door, and let yourself in. Give yourself a hug and a warm drink. Treat yourself like you would an honored and loved guest.

Practice compassion toward yourself. There are many ways to practice self-compassion. For more information on this, it's worth checking out this website: https://self-compassion.org/. For now, here's one practice that we find helpful: Sit in a comfortable position, and place your hand on your upper chest. Feel the warmth of your hand on your chest and notice the mild sensation of pressure. Now extend warm wishes to yourself by saying silently to yourself, *May I be at ease. May I be content with my life. May I experience joy. May I feel safe and secure.* Remain in that position, mindfully repeating these words as many times as you like. See if you notice a sense of warmth or kindness toward yourself. You might feel this sensation in your chest or elsewhere. It's also okay if you don't feel anything. The idea is to act as if you feel warmth and compassion toward yourself. You might have to practice many times before you notice those feelings arising.

MOVING FORWARD

This chapter taught you a number of different skills you can use to avoid making things worse when you feel shame. These skills fall within the broader category of DBT distress tolerance skills, and we specifically covered the skills of distraction and radical acceptance.

As with all of the skills we cover, distraction and radical acceptance require practice. Practice them even when you're not feeling much shame so you'll be more ready to use them when you do.

Also, remember that distress tolerance skills won't always make you feel better. Sometimes they'll take the edge off your shame; and, at other times, they'll reduce your suffering; and at yet other times, you might not notice much of a difference. If you don't notice much of a difference, then ask yourself, *Did I avoid doing anything that made things worse?* If the answer is yes, then the skills worked.

In this chapter, you learned skills to avoid making things worse when you're experiencing shame. In the next chapter, you'll learn skills that you can use to manage the upsetting thoughts and judgments about yourself that accompany shame.

CHAPTER 7

How to Check the Facts
When It Comes to Shame

In this chapter, we help you deal with one of the main problems with shame: negative beliefs and judgments about yourself. You're unlikely to experience shame if you don't think that you're bad, flawed, or unacceptable in some way. Most of the time, these types of negative self-judgments fuel shame. For this reason, one of the best ways to manage shame is to use skills to deal with these kinds of thoughts. That's what the DBT skill of *checking the facts* (Linehan 2015) is all about.

THOUGHTS THAT ACCOMPANY AND PROMPT SHAME

You might recall from chapters 1 and 3 that all emotions are made up of physical, cognitive, and behavioral components. These components work together like sections of a symphony to create the music of your emotions. The style, instruments, and tempo of the cognitive section influence the behavioral and physical sections, and vice versa. As you probably remember, the specialty of the cognitive section—the focus of the cognitive component of any emotion—is thoughts about yourself, the world, your life, and other people.

Many emotions have characteristic types of thoughts that tend to go along with them. Here are some examples:

- **Anger:** Thoughts about unfairness, injustice, or being threatened often are accompanied by anger. Thoughts that something is getting in your way or preventing you from achieving an important goal can also accompany and fuel anger.

- **Anxiety:** Thoughts often accompanying anxiety consist of worry or concerns about negative or uncertain events. If you find yourself worrying a lot, there's a good chance that you're feeling anxious.

- **Fear:** Similar to anxiety, fear usually goes along with thoughts about danger to your health, life, or well-being. Fear is there to protect you from danger, so when you think you're in danger, you'll feel afraid and want to protect yourself.

- **Sadness:** Thoughts accompanying sadness often have themes of loss or disappointment. You might have thoughts about being alone, loved ones being gone or unavailable, or things not working out as you would have liked.

Shame tends to go along with global negative thoughts and judgments about yourself. Judgments and thoughts are global when they are very broad and general. The thought, for example, that you're a "bad person" is a global judgment of yourself as a person. It's general and not specific to any particular situation.

We consider shame to be a "self-conscious" emotion because it's one of those emotions that usually arises when you're thinking of yourself in a particularly negative way. Common types of shame-related thoughts include these:

- thoughts that you're bad, worthless, or deficient in some way

- thoughts that you're unacceptable to yourself or others

- thoughts that you'll be rejected by others

- thoughts that you're undeserving of good things in life

As you can probably see, these thoughts tend to be both negative and global, or overly general. In fact, shame-related thoughts are often so general that it's hard to know what to make of them. It's like the shame section is repeating the same piece of music with only one or two instruments, all in the minor key, and the music is saying something like "I'm bad" over and over. What on earth does it really mean that you're "bad"? Are you really bad in all ways, at everything, in every situation? Unlikely. Yet these thoughts tell you it's so, and carrying the weight of them can be crushing and demoralizing. Moreover, when it comes to shame, the cognitive section takes the lead, resulting in a rather depressing and painful symphony.

In this chapter you'll learn how you can use the skill of checking the facts to get a handle on global, negative, shame-related thoughts and judgments. As illustrated in figure 1 (following), shame-related thoughts, feelings, and behaviors can influence each other in a vicious cycle, with certain thoughts and actions fueling more and more shame. You can also see from figure 1 that checking the facts helps address the cognitive piece of this picture, whereas the skill of opposite action (which you'll learn about in chapter 8) helps address the behavioral part. Checking the facts can help you identify shame-related thoughts when they arise, consider whether these thoughts really fit the situation (spoiler alert: they pretty much never do!), and find other, more flexible and compassionate ways to think about yourself.

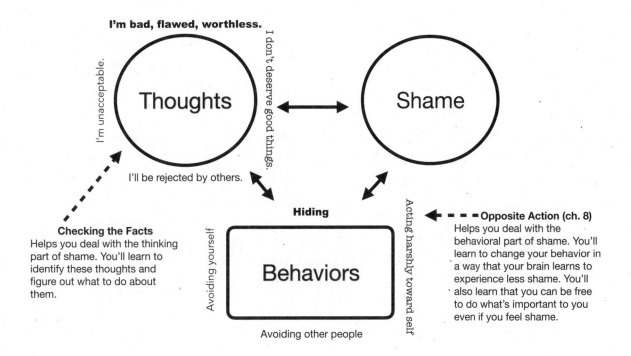

STEPS TO PRACTICE CHECKING THE FACTS

If you have read Dr. Marsha Linehan's *DBT Skills Training Manual,* 2nd edition (Linehan 2015), or have ever been in a DBT skills group, you might know that checking the facts is one of the more complicated skills, with several steps. Rest assured, though, we'll break down this skill into four simple steps so you can begin to practice it and get some relief from shame-related thoughts. Here are the steps:

Step 1: Describe the situation accurately and nonjudgmentally.

Step 2: Label the emotions and the thoughts going through your mind.

Step 3: Consider whether you're assuming a threat or catastrophe.

Step 4: Practice considering realistic outcomes.

Let's go through each of these steps, with some examples and exercises to help you work through and get used to them.

Step 1: Describe the Situation Accurately and Nonjudgmentally

When you experience an episode of shame, as soon as possible, write out a description of the situation. Start by writing the first description that comes to mind, without censoring or leaving anything out. Then, take a little break, come back to your description, and ask yourself if you've included any negative global statements or judgments about yourself or others. If you have, cross those out, and rewrite your description without them.

Below is an example of Molly's first description of a situation that brought up shame for her. Molly struggles with social anxiety and shame. She has been trying to get out and be more social, but whenever she does, she judges herself harshly afterward and ends up in a miserable shame spiral. Example Description #1 is Molly's first attempt at describing the situation.

EXAMPLE DESCRIPTION #1

I finally dragged myself out of my apartment to go to Shane's party around 8:30. When I got there, of course I was forty-five minutes late—typical. I walked in and everyone was staring at me. I just threw my clothes on and looked really frumpy; everyone else looked so much better. I immediately glommed onto Shane and his partner, because I can't mingle at parties, but I spent the whole time talking about that new podcast that I love, and people were probably getting sick of me. I wandered around for a bit, hovered awkwardly at the food and drink table, and then went back out to try to make small talk. My voice was wavering and ridiculous sounding, and I didn't have anything to say to anyone. After mingling awkwardly for a little longer, I left early, came home, and curled into a ball on the couch. I'm such an idiot. They'll probably never want to invite me back again.

In the following section, we've crossed out the statements that we found to be especially judgmental, global, or negative. Before you look, go back to description #1 and see if you can do that yourself. Compare yours to ours, and see if you caught all of the same statements.

> I ~~finally dragged myself out of~~ my apartment to go to Shane's party around 8:30. When I got there, ~~of course~~ I was forty-five minutes late~~—typical~~. I walked in ~~and everyone was staring at me. I just threw~~ my clothes on ~~and looked really frumpy; everyone else looked so much better.~~ I ~~immediately glommed onto~~ Shane and his partner, ~~because I can't mingle at parties,~~ but I ~~spent the whole time talking about~~ that new podcast that I love, ~~and people were probably getting sick of me.~~ I wandered around for a bit, ~~hovered awkwardly~~ at the food and drink table, and then went back out to try to make small talk. My voice was wavering ~~and ridiculous sounding, and I didn't have anything to say to anyone.~~ After mingling ~~awkwardly~~ for a little longer, I left early, came home, and curled into a ball on the couch. ~~I'm such an idiot. They'll probably never want to invite me back again.~~

Here's a revised version of Molly's description:

> ## EXAMPLE #1 REVISION
>
> I left my apartment to go to Shane's party around 8:30. When I got there, I was forty-five minutes late. I walked in and saw some people looking my way and felt anxious. I wasn't too happy with what I was wearing (I didn't leave myself much time to change). I remember thinking that many of the people looked really stylish. I hung out with Shane and his partner for a while, as I was anxious about mingling. I worried that I spent too much time talking about the new podcast that I love. I wandered around for a bit, spent some time at the food and drink table, and then went back out to try to make small talk. My voice was wavering. I was afraid people could tell I was nervous, and I had a hard time coming up with things to say. After mingling for a little longer, I left early, came home, and curled into a ball on the couch. I started to worry that they might not have enjoyed having me over.

We're hoping you can see that even though the revised version gets rid of all of the negative, global judgments and statements, it's not all wine and roses. This was a hard thing for Molly to do, and we wanted our revision to capture that. So we left out the judgments and described the difficulty and anxiety Molly experienced. We also aimed to write Example #1 Revision in a way that was a little kinder and more compassionate.

Okay, now it's your turn. Use exercise 7.1 to write out your first practice description of a situation in which you felt shame. (If you prefer, you can download this exercise at http://www.newharbinger. com/49616.)

Exercise 7.1: Practice Description #1

Describe a situation in which you felt shame. Just use whatever words come to mind. Don't edit or censor yourself. If judgments come to mind, that's fine, just write them down. This is just your first draft.

_____

_____

_____

_____

_____

_____

_____

Having written your first description, go back and cross out all of the statements about yourself (or your life, or others) that are negative, global, or judgmental. Take a good look at what you've crossed out, and in exercise 7.2, write a revised version that is more accurate, and maybe a little kinder and more compassionate. (If you prefer, you can download this exercise at http://www.newhar binger.com/49616.) If you find it needs more work, go ahead and revise it again. This step takes time. Don't expect or aim for perfection.

Exercise 7.2: Practice Revision #1

Describe a situation in which you felt shame. This time, leave out the stuff you crossed out, and write a revised version that is more accurate and maybe a little kinder and more compassionate.

_____

_____

_____

_____

_____

_____

_____

Try exercises 7.1 and 7.2 a couple of times with different situations. See if you can become more aware of negative global thoughts and judgments about yourself. Once you get some practice, you'll probably notice these thoughts more quickly. You might even notice when you're thinking them in your daily life. If this happens, tell yourself, *That's a judgment,* or *That's just shame talking,* or something like that. Then, try to restate the thought in a way that's more accurate, kinder, and more compassionate, just as you did with the exercise above.

Step 2: Label the Emotions and the Thoughts Going Through Your Mind

Another important step in checking the facts is to label the emotions and thoughts going through your mind. In chapter 1, we provided you with information on what shame is and its different components, and in chapter 3, we helped you understand your own patterns of shame. We're going to assume, then, that you've had some practice and are getting better at noticing the signs of shame when they come along. For this step, we'll revisit a little of what we reviewed in chapter 5 on mindfulness. Remember how we discussed the importance of labeling a thought as a thought? That's part of what we'll focus on here.

So, how do you label shame-related thoughts going through your mind as just thoughts when these thoughts are so painful? Well, it helps to find a comfortable place to sit or lie down. Next, step back in your mind and try to notice what you're thinking. For guidance on how to do this, please refer to exercise 5.1 (Practicing Teflon Mind) in chapter 5.

Let's return to the example of Molly to see how she identified shame-related thoughts. When Molly arrived home after the party, she felt like curling up into a ball and disappearing. She felt a sensation of heat in her face and a sinking feeling in her stomach—signs of shame for Molly.

Knowing that there was a good chance that negative thoughts about herself were fueling her shame, Molly decided to get a handle on what she was thinking. She took a few deep breaths, put away her phone, turned off the TV, sat in a comfortable position, and listened to the words going through her mind. These are the words Molly heard:

- *You're so awkward and weird.*

- *You don't know how to talk to people.*

- *People don't like you.*

- *They're probably talking right now about how they're not going to invite you back.*

Thoughts also come in the form of images:

- Molly saw herself arriving at the door with clothing that didn't seem as stylish as what other people were wearing.

- Molly saw herself standing awkwardly by the food and drink table, looking down, and being alone.

You might notice that these thoughts that Molly noticed were global negative judgments of herself, with the theme that she's weird and unlikeable.

Okay, now it's your turn. Use exercise 7.3 to step back, notice, and describe the thoughts and images going through your mind. (You can download this exercise at http://www.newharbinger.com/49616.)

Exercise 7.3: Noticing and Listing Judgments

Find a comfortable and quiet place, and take a few deep breaths. Come back to the situation that you described earlier. Put yourself in that situation in your mind. Try to notice what words and images are going through your mind. Watch for global, general judgments of yourself; those types of thoughts are most strongly related to shame. Make a list of the judgments that come to mind.

_____

_____

_____

_____

_____

_____

_____

Once you've listed these judgments, you might find yourself feeling a little more shame. That's normal. As we've mentioned, these are the types of thoughts that bring up shame; therefore, getting in touch with them could bring up some shame in the moment. We recommend that you use the skills you learned in chapter 5 to take a step back from these thoughts and remind yourself that they are just judgments your mind has come up with. Tell yourself, *These are thoughts (albeit painful ones), not facts.*

Step 3: Consider Whether You're Assuming a Threat or Catastrophe

Another step in checking the facts is to ask yourself whether you're assuming that the situation that brought up your shame comes with some kind of danger. That's what we mean by "threat" or "catastrophe." Somewhere in your mind, you might be thinking the situation is dangerous to you. When it comes to emotions like fear, for example, people often assume that the situation is threatening to their well-being or health. People who are afraid of high places might assume that they will fall to their death. People who are afraid of speaking in public might assume that people will criticize them or judge them in some way.

Shame can also come with assumptions that a situation may have very negative outcomes. When it comes to shame, the negative outcomes often have to do with social rejection: the idea that people will abandon or reject you because of who you are or something you have done.

This is what Molly came up with when she asked herself if she was assuming a threat.

> I realized I was thinking that Shane would stop inviting me to do things. He wouldn't want to hang out with me anymore because I embarrassed him in front of his other friends, and because I'm weird and no fun. I was also worried he'd want to stop being my friend altogether.

Use exercise 7.4 to practice determining whether you're assuming a threat and then describing it if you are. (If you prefer, you can download this exercise from http://www.newharbinger.com/49616.)

Exercise 7.4: Are You Assuming a Threat?

Consider the situation you've described in the previous exercises. Think about whether something seems dangerous or threatening to you. Maybe you're worried that people won't like you or want to be with you, or that they'll reject you. Maybe you're worried that there's something wrong with you and this means you won't achieve important goals, such as work or school goals. See if you can identify something that seems threatening about the situation, and describe it below.

_____

_____

_____

_____

_____

Once you've got an idea of the threat, another step to take, if you're willing, is to dive even deeper and ask if you might be assuming a catastrophe. A *threat* is a negative consequence that might happen, and a *catastrophe* is just what it sounds like: a terrible, horrendous negative consequence—the worst-case scenario. In Molly's case, the threat might be that Shane will not want to spend time with her anymore. The catastrophe might be that she'll be left completely alone, with no friends at all, and this will lead to misery and depression.

How did Molly figure out whether she's assuming a catastrophe? She kept asking herself the question "Then what?" until she arrived at the worst-case scenario.

Here's Molly's example:

Shane won't invite me to get together anymore. *Then what?*

He'll realize things are more fun without me, and that I'm embarrassing to have around. *Then what?*

He'll realize I'm fundamentally weird and stop wanting to be friends with me. *Then what?*

My one other friend will realize the same, and I'll be left completely alone with no friends at all, sitting in my apartment watching TV, lonely and without any support. *Then what?*

I'll be miserable and depressed.

Try this out yourself, using exercise 7.5. (If you prefer, you can download the exercise at http://www.newharbinger.com/49616.)

Exercise 7.5: What's the Catastrophe You're Worried About?

Pick one threat you wrote down for exercise 7.4 and ask yourself, *Then what?* until you arrive at the worst-case scenario, or the catastrophe.

Describe the threat.

_____

_____

Then what? Describe.

_____

_____

Then what? Describe.

_____

_____

Then what? Describe.

_____

_____

Then what? Describe.

_____

_____

Once you've pinpointed any assumed threats or catastrophes, you're probably wondering where to go from there. One approach is to go back to the skills we reviewed in chapter 5 on mindfulness strategies for shame. Use some of the exercises in that chapter to allow yourself to experience these thoughts and let them come and go. Let go of them and see them as thoughts and not facts.

Step 4: Practice Considering Realistic Outcomes

Another way to deal with threats and catastrophes is to consider what the most realistic outcomes might be. What's most likely to happen? Is it really likely that Molly's friend Shane will stop being her friend altogether because she was anxious at a party? When Molly gave this some thought, she came up with the following description of the most realistic outcome:

Shane has stuck with me for a long time, he knows me well, and we're really close. I've been there for him, and he's been there for me. He's unlikely to stop inviting me just because I had a hard time at the party. Even though I was anxious, I didn't do anything really problematic like insult or criticize anyone. Nobody asked me to leave or told me I was annoying them. He'd really have no reason to not invite me back. In fact, the most realistic consequence might be that he'll be supportive of me: if I were to tell him I was really anxious but went to the party anyway, he'd probably be proud of me and happy that I came.

Now, thinking of and describing the most realistic outcome is not easy to do, especially if you're feeling strong shame (or other emotions). Strong emotions can make it hard to think clearly, and you have to be able to think clearly to consider realistic outcomes. Before you try to do this, we'd recommend that you check in on how intense your shame is right now. If your shame is very intense, consider using some of the skills we described in chapter 6 to bring your emotions to a more manageable level—a level where you can access your own wisdom and think clearly. Then, in exercise 7.6, describe the most realistic outcomes of the shame-related situation you've been working on in this chapter. (If you prefer, you can download this exercise at http://www.newharbinger.com/49616.)

Exercise 7.6: What's the Most Realistic Outcome?

Using Molly's example as a guide, write out the most likely outcome of your shame-related situation. Think about what's most likely to happen. One tip for doing this is to assume others have good intentions and to think of yourself with compassion. If you do these two things, you'll probably come up with a more realistic outcome.

_____

_____

_____

_____

_____

_____

MOVING FORWARD

In this chapter, we reviewed ways that you can work with thoughts related to shame. Common thinking patterns related to shame include global negative thoughts and judgments about yourself. The DBT skill of checking the facts is made to address these kinds of thoughts.

We reviewed four key steps for checking the facts: (1) describe the situation, (2) label emotions and thoughts, (3) ask if you're assuming a threat or catastrophe, and (4) consider realistic outcomes. You might have found that it wasn't easy to work on these steps. Checking the facts gets you in touch with some pretty upsetting thoughts about yourself. Like many upsetting things in life, though, we have to face these thoughts before we can do something about them. We hope that you've gotten off to a good start in tackling one of the most challenging aspects of the experience of shame. We believe that the more practice you get, the more often you'll think of yourself with compassion and kindness.

In chapter 8, we cover another important DBT skill—opposite action. Instead of working with your thoughts to manage shame, opposite action involves changing your behavior to become freer from shame. Like checking the facts, opposite action requires a lot of practice, but we think that you'll find it to be one of the most important tools in your journey toward becoming freer from shame and its grip on your life.

CHAPTER 8

Using Opposite Action to Reduce Shame

Now that you've learned all about the DBT skill of checking the facts and how this applies to shame, it's time to turn our attention toward the DBT skill that's the most helpful for regulating emotions that don't fit the facts. As you learned in chapter 2, DBT contains all kinds of different skills for regulating emotions. However, many of these skills are most helpful when emotions are adaptive and functional, or serve a useful purpose. For example, when you're feeling sad, it can be very helpful to try to understand the function of that emotion and the information it's providing you, as well as to allow yourself to fully experience that emotion. Likewise, when your emotions are helpful and fit the facts, it can be very useful to use skills like problem solving and acceptance.

As we've discussed throughout this book, however, shame is different from most other emotions we experience because it usually isn't helpful or adaptive in any way. If your shame tells you that you're a bad person, or unworthy of love or care, or undeserving of anything positive, then this isn't a very useful emotion. Indeed, because shame often stems from negative judgments and evaluations of yourself as a person, the information it tends to provide in those moments is that you are flawed, faulty, or otherwise not acceptable as you are—information that is never helpful! Therefore, one of the most helpful skills for managing shame is the DBT emotion regulation skill for changing emotions that are not helpful and don't fit the facts: opposite action (Linehan 1993b).

As you may remember from earlier chapters in this book, the DBT skill of opposite action is the ideal skill for reducing emotions that are not helpful and do not fit the facts. And shame is often the perfect example of this type of emotion. Therefore, when you're experiencing shame and looking for an effective skill to help you reduce this emotion, opposite action is an excellent choice.

THE NUTS AND BOLTS OF OPPOSITE ACTION

Opposite action involves doing the opposite of what the emotion is telling you to do, or acting opposite to what the emotion prompts you to do (that is, the action urges associated with that emotion). Basically, because all emotions are made up of physical, cognitive, and behavioral components, one way to modify or regulate an emotion is to change one of those components. In the case of opposite action, you are changing the behavioral component of the emotion by doing the opposite of what your emotion tells you to do. When you do this, the emotion tends to change and become less intense, either in the moment or over time with repeated practice.

To make sure you understand how this skill works (before you try to use it to help manage your shame), it may be helpful to think about how it would work to regulate other emotions. Consider the example of phobias, or intense and unrealistic fears of objects or situations. Because the fear that goes along with phobias is excessive, unhelpful, and doesn't fit the facts (for example, intense fears of any kind of spider, even if it is not dangerous), opposite action is an ideal skill for managing and reducing this fear. The action urges that accompany this fear are generally to avoid the feared object or situation. So, people with a spider phobia may avoid thinking about, looking at, or being near spiders, and people with a phobia of heights may avoid going to the upper floors of multistory buildings, climbing high ladders, going out on upper-level terraces, or even looking out windows that are not on the ground floor.

Therefore, the opposite actions for these action urges involve actively approaching the feared object or situation and coming into contact with it. For example, opposite action for a spider phobia could involve looking at pictures of spiders, watching videos of spiders, listening to someone talk about spiders, reading a book about spiders, being in the same room as a spider, or even touching a nonpoisonous spider—anything that increases contact with the feared object. By acting opposite to the urge to avoid anything having to do with spiders, you are changing the behavioral component of the emotion of fear, which in turn regulates the fear and lessens its intensity. The same principle applies when using opposite action to reduce shame, although the action urges and relevant opposite actions are different.

Now that you have a better understanding of the opposite action skill, we can apply this skill to shame. Because opposite action requires you to act opposite to the action urges of an emotion, the first step in using this skill is identifying the action urges that go along with shame for you. You already started this process in chapter 3 when you learned how to recognize and identify feelings of shame. One of the exercises you completed in that chapter focused on identifying the action urges that go along with shame for you. Thus, to help you use the opposite action skill to reduce your shame, start by reviewing the action urges you identified in exercise 3.5 of chapter 3 and writing those into the form for exercise 8.3 at the end of this chapter.

OPPOSITE ACTIONS FOR COMMON SHAME ACTION URGES

After you've identified all of the action urges that go along with shame for you, the next step is to figure out how to act opposite to these action urges. The opposite actions that will be most helpful for reducing your shame in the moment will depend on the specific action urges you're experiencing right then. To get you thinking about this, we will review some of the most common action urges associated with shame and share specific strategies for acting opposite to these urges. As we've discussed before, the most common action urges associated with shame include hiding/avoiding, self-punishing, and beating yourself up or speaking critically to yourself. Helpful opposite actions for each of these action urges are reviewed below.

Opposite Actions for the Action Urge of Hiding/Avoiding

This particular action urge can take a number of different forms, which means that the opposite actions for these urges will vary as well. For some people, the urge to hide means literally wanting to hide away from everyone—for example, by staying in bed under the covers all day or not leaving the house.

If your action urge is to stay in bed, the opposite actions include getting out of bed (even if you don't feel like it!), getting showered and dressed for the day (with a bonus opposite action if you put on clothes that are comforting to you, or that make you feel good about yourself), and making sure not to hang out in your bedroom after you wake up.

If your action urge is to hide from the world by not leaving your home, then possible opposite actions include running an errand outside of your home, making plans with someone to do something during the day, eating at a coffee shop or restaurant, going to the store, or taking a walk outside. Basically, anything you can do to get out of your home will count as opposite action. The key is to not let yourself hide out from others in your room or home. As difficult as it may be to resist urges to avoid others, doing so will help you reduce your feelings of shame.

The urges to hide that go along with shame can also involve urges to hide parts of yourself, your identity, or your thoughts and feelings from others. In these cases, the hiding is a bit more subtle. People can hide parts of themselves even if they are with other people or actively socialize with others. In fact, on the surface, it may be hard to recognize this as hiding since this particular action urge does not involve avoiding spending time with others. The problem, though, is that hiding parts of yourself and your identity from others can actually increase feelings of shame and reinforce the belief that you are flawed in some way. Therefore, it can be really helpful to practice opposite action for these urges as well.

If you have urges to hide parts of yourself or your identity from others, the opposite actions for these urges include sharing those parts of yourself with others. For example, if you have urges to hide some part of your identity from others, like your gender identity or sexual orientation, consider sharing this with a trusted friend, therapist, or family member. If even the thought of doing this makes you feel anxious or unsafe, that's completely understandable. Sharing this type of information with someone else can be scary, especially if you've been rejected, discriminated against, or harmed for doing so in the past. The key here is to share this information with someone you believe will be open to and affirming of your identity. You don't need to share all aspects of yourself with everyone in your life (although you certainly can if you want to!). Who you choose to share these parts of yourself with is completely up to you, and it's perfectly acceptable if that means sharing these parts of yourself with only one person or many.

In order for this skill to be helpful, you just need to act opposite to the urge to hide by opening up and sharing who you are with someone. So, think about who in your life would be open and receptive to hearing about this aspect of your identity, and write their name here.

Name: _____

Then, try sharing this part of you with just that one person to start. Even that will go a long way in helping you reduce your shame.

Likewise, if you tend to hide your feelings and thoughts from others, make it a point to start sharing these. If someone asks for your opinion about something, tell them what you think. If you're feeling sad or anxious, tell someone about it. Take some time to think about some people in your life who might be open to hearing about your feelings and thoughts, and accepting of those. Write their names here.

Name: _____

Name: _____

Name: _____

Opening up with others about your feelings and thoughts can help regulate your shame and teach you that it is okay to express yourself.

Another form that this action urge can take is the urge to hide some of your experiences from others. As we discussed in chapter 1, past experiences, particularly traumatic experiences, can be a major cause of shame for some people. And, in these cases, the action urges that go along with shame include hiding those experiences from others and trying to keep them a secret. As you probably guessed, the opposite action for that urge is to tell someone about these experiences. As scary as this may be, telling someone what happened to you and opening up about your experience can be incredibly helpful for reducing shame. The more you are able to talk about it—even if only with a couple of trusted friends or family members, or your therapist—the less shame you will feel about this experience. If the idea of sharing an experience you've kept hidden from others is overwhelming or daunting, keep in mind that it's okay to start small. You don't have to share all details of this experience right away. Just telling someone something about it, or mentioning that you've had that type of experience in general, will help reduce your shame.

Mary's Story

Although Mary had experienced several traumas in her life, the one that continued to affect her the most was the sexual assault she experienced when she was in college. There was so much about this experience that made it complicated. She had agreed to go out on a date with someone from class and had a couple of glasses of wine at dinner—more than she normally drank. Then, she agreed to go back to his apartment after dinner to watch a movie. When he assaulted her later that night, she wondered if it was her fault and if she had led him on in some way.

The shame from that experience and from blaming herself was incredibly intense and was starting to influence all aspects of her life and her self-esteem. Although she was seeing a therapist for depression, she hadn't yet shared this experience with her therapist, and was scared that her fears that she was to blame would be confirmed.

After learning about opposite action for shame, she wondered if talking about this experience and telling her therapist could help her with her shame. So, during her next session, she let her therapist know that she had been sexually assaulted. As she said the words, she noticed that her heart rate increased, her voice wavered, and she was having urges to look away. Instead, she looked her therapist in the eyes and told her. When her therapist responded with compassion and concern and immediately told her that it was not her fault, Mary immediately felt better and could feel some of the shame associated with this experience beginning to lift. Over time, she talked more about the experience in her sessions, including the shame associated with it. And, over time, her shame reduced considerably until she could talk about it with only fleeting feelings of shame.

Now, when it comes to any of these opposite actions for the urge to hide, there's one other step that can make these actions even more powerful in combating shame. Specifically, that step has to do with *how* you do the opposite actions, or the way you go about spending time around others, or socializing with others, and sharing parts of yourself or your experiences with others. Basically, in order to get the greatest "dose" of opposite action, it's important that you throw yourself completely into these actions and counter any urges to hide in more subtle ways. Even if you're spending time with or opening up to others, it's still possible to hide in other ways, such as by avoiding eye contact, speaking softly, or trying to fade into the background or sink into yourself.

Therefore, when you do the opposite actions we just discussed, it's important to do them in ways that are opposite to these more subtle urges to hide as well. When you're spending time with people, make sure to keep your head up and look people in the eyes when you speak to them. When you're sharing a part of yourself or your experiences, make sure to maintain eye contact, sit or stand up straight, and speak in a normal volume (not whispering). The more that you interact and communicate with other people in a self-assured manner, the more you will benefit from these actions and experience a reduction in your shame.

Opposite Actions for the Action Urge of Self-Punishing

One of the main action urges that often goes along with shame is to self-punish. Because shame arises when people judge themselves as flawed, faulty, or unworthy, it often goes along with the urge to punish oneself for some perceived flaw or wrongdoing. And this makes sense. If you think there is something wrong with you, it's only natural that you would want to punish yourself in some way. The problem with this is that punishing yourself will only intensify your shame in the long run and further reinforce the idea that you are unworthy or flawed in some way. Therefore, acting opposite to these urges is one of the most helpful skills you can use. There are a number of ways you can act opposite to the urge to punish yourself.

Do something nice for yourself. Even if you feel like you aren't deserving of anything positive, you can act as if you are deserving by doing something nice for yourself. Give yourself a gift, treat yourself to your favorite meal or snack, watch your favorite television show or movie, or practice some of the skills for taking care of your body that we described in chapter 4. Acting as if you are deserving of positive things is one way to reduce feelings of shame.

Practice self-soothing. Another great way to counteract urges to punish yourself is to do something to soothe or comfort yourself instead. In DBT, self-soothing skills are a way to comfort yourself by introducing calming and soothing sensations to your five senses: touch, taste, smell, sight, and hearing (Linehan 1993b, 2015). The goal is to create gentle sensations that calm you. There are many sensations that people find soothing and comforting (Linehan 1993b, 2015). Many of these were taken from our book *The Dialectical Behavior Therapy Skills Workbook for Anxiety* (Chapman, Gratz, and Tull 2011).

Touch

- Take a warm bubble bath or hot shower, or sit in a hot tub. Focus on the feeling of the water against your skin.

- Sit outside and relax in the sun, focusing on the warmth of the sun on your skin.

- Introduce sensations that soothe your body and feel good against your skin. Put on soft clothing, such as a fuzzy sweater, flannel shirt, warm fleece, or cotton sweatshirt or T-shirt. Focus on the feeling of the fabric against your skin.

- Get a massage, or give yourself a massage.

- Pet your cat or dog (or other animal), focusing on the feel of the fur against your skin.

- Hug a friend or loved one.

- Wrap yourself up in a warm, fluffy blanket and curl up on a comfortable chair or in bed.

- Sit in front of a fire and focus on the warmth you feel.

Taste

- Eat your favorite comfort food, such as sushi, freshly baked bread, mashed potatoes, fudge, or macaroni and cheese.

- Sip a cup of hot cocoa, tea, or some other hot drink. Focus on the warmth that spreads through your body as you drink these.

- On a hot day, eat or drink something cold, like a popsicle, ice cream bar, or iced drink.

- Eat a piece of fresh fruit and really focus on the flavors.

Smell

- Burn incense or light a scented candle and focus on the scents that are released.

- Apply scented lotion to your skin and inhale the aroma.

- Go to a flower shop, botanical garden, or arboretum and breathe in the scents of the flowers.

- Inhale the aroma of lavender or vanilla.

- Go outside and breathe in fresh air.

- Bake cookies or fresh bread and breathe in the aroma. Smell fresh coffee beans or brew fresh coffee.

- Cut fresh herbs or open jars of spices and breathe in deeply.

- Light a fire and focus on the smell of the smoke and burning wood.

Sight

- Look at pictures of loved ones or a favorite vacation spot.

- Look at pictures of things you find relaxing, such as a beach, a sunset, or a beautiful mountain.

- Go to the beach and watch the waves hit the sand.

- Watch a sunset.

- Watch clouds in the sky or leaves rustling in the breeze.

- Watch your pet or children play or sleep.

- Watch the flames of a fire or candle move and dance in the air.

Hearing

- Listen to relaxing music, birds singing, or children playing.

- Take a walk through the woods or around your neighborhood and listen to the sounds of nature.

- Sit outside at dusk and listen to the crickets.

- Go to the beach and listen to the sound of waves crashing on the shore.

- Light a fire and listen to the pop and crackle of the wood.

Exercise 8.1: Identifying Self-Soothing Strategies

Now that you've learned more about the self-soothing skills of DBT, see if you can come up with some self-soothing skills that would be especially comforting for you. Focus on each of your five senses and different things that you find most soothing. See if you can identify five different activities for each sense. (This exercise is available for download at http://www.newharbinger.com/49616.)

Touch

_____

_____

_____

_____

_____

Taste

_____

_____

_____

_____

_____

Smell

_____

_____

_____

_____

Sight

_____

_____

_____

_____

Hearing

_____

_____

_____

_____

Now that you have identified some self-soothing skills that may work for you, you can use these skills the next time you have an urge to punish yourself. When you notice this urge, use one of these skills instead. The more you do this, the more your shame will reduce.

Just as we recommended doing the opposite actions for hiding in a particular way in order to make them most helpful, it is important to practice opposite actions for self-punishing in a particular way too. Specifically, in order to benefit the most from these skills, make sure to use the DBT skill of throwing yourself completely into whatever you are doing in the moment (Linehan 1993b, 2015) to focus all of your attention on the experience of taking care of yourself in these ways. So, as you do something nice for yourself, focus on how that feels in the moment and what that experience is like. Similarly, as you practice the self-soothing skills described above, be sure to focus all of your attention completely on your sensations. Stay in the moment. If you find yourself getting distracted, notice that, and then turn your attention back to your experience in the moment. If negative self-judgments arise, simply notice them and then bring your attention back to the experience of taking care of yourself.

Opposite Actions for the Action Urge of Beating Yourself Up or Speaking Critically to Yourself

In the same way that negative self-judgments can lead to urges to punish yourself in some way, these same judgments can lead to urges to criticize yourself or beat yourself up. Many people who struggle with shame find that they have a tendency to be hard on themselves for the smallest mistakes, or even for simply being human! Basically, anytime they perceive themselves as not being perfect can be a cue for shame and lead to urges to berate or criticize themselves. If this is the case for you, then you can probably relate to just how exhausting and painful it can be to constantly feel urges to criticize yourself. You have probably also experienced how giving into these urges only intensifies your shame and makes you feel worse about yourself. That's why opposite action is such a helpful skill to use in situations like this.

When you find yourself wanting to beat yourself up or be self-critical, do the opposite of this instead. In this case, the opposite of this urge is to treat yourself with kindness, compassion, and respect. There are a number of different ways to treat yourself with kindness and compassion.

One way is to use the self-soothing skills we discussed in the previous section. Although these skills can be a way of acting opposite to urges to punish yourself, they can also be a way to act opposite to urges to beat yourself up. You can think of the self-soothing skills as a way to treat yourself with compassion by doing things that are comforting and soothing to you. So, any of the skills you identified in exercise 8.1 will also be helpful here.

Another way to act opposite to urges to self-criticize is to speak to yourself with kindness and respect. Rather than criticizing yourself, speak to yourself in a kind way, avoiding any judgmental language or harsh words. Some people find it helpful to speak to themselves like they would speak to their best friend. Think about what you would say if your best friend came to you and said that they had done something wrong or messed up in some way. How would you respond to your friend? Write down three things you might say to your friend.

_____

_____

_____

Approach yourself in this same way, speaking to yourself exactly as if you were speaking to your friend.

Another strategy is to think about how someone you are close to and trust would respond to you. For example, if you have a therapist you trust, think about how your therapist would respond and what they would say to you if you said you were a terrible person or had done something wrong. Try to echo their words and tone when speaking to yourself. Write down three things they might say to you.

_____

_____

_____

Now, don't be surprised if this feels quite uncomfortable at first. This is definitely one of those skills that gets easier with practice. If you're used to speaking to yourself in a critical or unkind way, approaching yourself with compassion and speaking to yourself with kindness is probably going to feel awkward, and could even bring up some distress or thoughts that you don't deserve to speak to yourself in this way. And that's okay. Changing these types of patterns takes time. What's most important is that you continue to practice this skill when you notice urges to criticize yourself, even if it feels awkward or uncomfortable. The more you practice speaking to yourself in these ways, the more natural it will become.

Another opposite action for this action urge is to focus your attention on your strengths and positive characteristics. Use the DBT mindfulness skills of noticing your experience and focusing attention on one thing at a time (Linehan 1993b, 2015) to focus all of your attention on the things you like about yourself and your positive qualities and behaviors. Think about all of your accomplishments and the things you're most proud of in your life. Take a step back and recognize these. Think about steps you've been taking to improve your life and gain more skills. Consider how you've been using the various skills you've learned from this book to lessen the hold shame has on your life. Focus on the parts of yourself that you appreciate. Write down three things that come to mind now.

_____

_____

_____

If your shame makes it hard to identify anything you like about yourself, focus on the things you do for others and the ways in which your actions have positive consequences for others. Alternatively, ask your friends, therapist, or loved ones to tell you what they think your positive qualities are and the things they value about you. Then, really focus your attention on taking in this information. Although it may feel awkward and uncomfortable at first, focusing your attention on all of your strengths and positive characteristics is an excellent way of acting opposite to the action urges to beat yourself up that go along with shame.

Brian's Story

Brian was having a terrible week at work. He had so many deadlines coming up and so many new tasks had been put on his plate that he was finding it challenging to get everything done and stay on top of things. In fact, yesterday he had forgotten about a deadline and ended up not getting some paperwork submitted on time. He had corrected that mistake today and been told that it wasn't a problem and all of the paperwork would be processed. However, he couldn't stop beating himself up for making the mistake. All day, he found himself being incredibly critical of everything he did and calling himself names like "stupid" and "imbecile." He just couldn't stop the shame from arising and influencing how he was treating himself.

Once he noticed that he was falling back into these old patterns, he remembered that taking care of himself physically could reduce vulnerability to shame, so he went to bed early to try to get a good night's sleep. When he woke up the next morning, however, he was still feeling terrible about himself and having a very difficult time not beating himself up for not being perfect at work. That's when he remembered the opposite action skills he had learned to help reduce shame by acting opposite to what it made him want to do.

Seeing that his shame was making him want to criticize himself and say mean things to himself, Brian decided to do the opposite of that and instead approach himself with kindness. He focused on everything he had accomplished the past month at work, and the positive feedback he'd received from his supervisor. He also practiced approaching his recent mistake with compassion—the same way he would if one of his coworkers had made the mistake. He told himself that everyone makes mistakes and that doesn't mean that he should judge himself as a terrible worker. To treat himself with kindness and compassion, he also stopped at his favorite coffee shop on the way to work and treated himself to his favorite special coffee drink, making sure to really focus on the experience of drinking it, and its warmth and sweet taste. By the time he pulled into work, he was feeling less ashamed and better able to tackle all of the things he needed to do that day.

PRACTICING OPPOSITE ACTION TO SHAME SKILLS

Now that you've learned about many of the different opposite action skills you can use to combat shame, it's time to put them into action! The next time you experience one of the shame action urges we discussed, including hiding, punishing yourself, or beating yourself up, try out one of the opposite action skills specific to that action urge. The key to these skills is to practice them as much as you can. As with many of the DBT skills we discuss in this book, opposite action skills can become easier and more natural over time. You just need to try them whenever your shame is making you want to do something that isn't helpful, like treating yourself poorly, hiding aspects of yourself and your experience from others, and avoiding others. The good news is that since there are so many different opposite action skills for shame, you have a number of different options to select from, depending on what works best for you. Therefore, the next step is to try out the various skills we discussed here and see how well they work for you. Use exercise 8.2 to determine the most helpful skills for you. (If you prefer, you can download the exercise at http://www.newharbinger.com/49616.)

Exercise 8.2: Trying Out Opposite Action Skills for Shame

Use this exercise to help you figure out which of the opposite action skills we reviewed in this chapter work best for you. First, rate the intensity of your shame on a scale of 0 (no shame at all) to 10 (the most intense shame ever) in the Shame Before column. Next, try out some of the opposite action skills listed in the left column. You can choose which skills to try depending on which of the action urges you're experiencing. After you use each skill, immediately rate your shame again on a scale from 0 to 10 in the Shame After column. After you have tried out some of these skills a few times, you might notice that some are more helpful to you than others in reducing your shame.

Opposite Action Skill	Shame Before (0 to 10)	Shame After (0 to 10)
Skills for the action urge of hiding/avoiding		
Avoid hiding out in your bed or home.		
Get out of the house and around people by running an errand, going for a walk outside, or going to a coffee shop or restaurant.		
Make plans to do something with someone else.		
Share a previously hidden part of yourself or your identity with a trusted friend, therapist, or loved one.		
Share your feelings and thoughts with others.		
Share an experience you've kept hidden with a trusted person in your life.		
Maintain eye contact with others and speak in a clear voice and normal volume.		
Sit or stand up straight; carry yourself in a self-assured manner.		

Opposite Action Skill	Shame Before (0 to 10)	Shame After (0 to 10)
Skills for the action urge of punishing yourself		
Do something nice for yourself.		
Use self-soothing skills to introduce comforting or relaxing sensations.		
Touch		
Taste		
Smell		
Sight		
Hearing		
Skills for the action urge of beating yourself up or criticizing yourself		
Treat yourself with compassion by doing things that are comforting for you.		
Touch		
Taste		
Smell		
Sight		
Hearing		
Speak to yourself with kindness and respect.		
Focus on your strengths and positive qualities.		

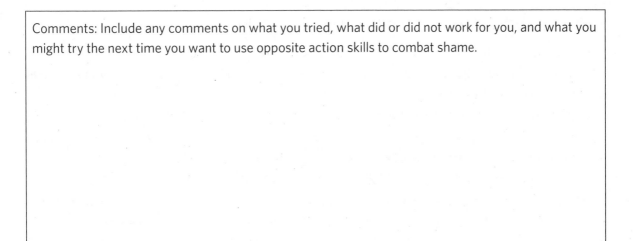

Comments: Include any comments on what you tried, what did or did not work for you, and what you might try the next time you want to use opposite action skills to combat shame.

INCORPORATING OPPOSITE ACTION INTO YOUR DAILY LIFE

Now that you have a better sense of how opposite action works and some of the specific opposite actions you can take to reduce shame, let's focus on identifying the particular opposite action skills that will be the best fit for the action urges that tend to accompany shame for you. At the beginning of this chapter, we asked you to take the information you learned in chapter 3 about the action urges you typically experience when you're feeling shame and write it in exercise 8.3. If you haven't done that yet, go ahead and do it now.

Some of your action urges are probably quite similar to some of those we discussed in this chapter, whereas others may be more specific to you. Now that you've identified your own personal action urges for shame, you can use the skills you learned in this chapter to identify how you can act opposite to those urges the next time you experience them. Remember, part of this is doing the exact opposite of what the shame is telling you to do and part of this is about how you do it—for example, by holding your head up high, looking people in the eye, speaking with confidence, and paying attention to positive and comforting experiences. Exercise 8.3 will help you figure out exactly what skills you can use to counteract the action urges that go along with shame for you. (If you prefer, you can download the exercise at http://www.newharbinger.com/49616.

Exercise 8.3: Using Opposite Action for Shame in Your Daily Life

This exercise will help you identify specific opposite action skills you can use depending on the action urges associated with shame for you. In the first column, write down the most common action urges that go along with shame for you, or what you tend to feel like doing when you are experiencing shame. Next, in the second column, write down the opposite actions for that action urge. Because this isn't always easy to figure out, we've included some more examples for you in the form below. Remember, though, the idea is to do the opposite of what you feel like doing. So, if you feel like avoiding people, make plans to spend time with people instead. If you feel like hiding a part of yourself, share that part of yourself with others. Finally, in the last column, rate how helpful the opposite action skill was in reducing your shame from 0 (not at all helpful, no reduction in shame) to 10 (extremely helpful, shame went way down).

Action Urges	Opposite Actions	Helpful? (0 to 10)
Isolate myself from others	Leave my house and go someplace where I can be around others and interact with them, like a coffee shop. Strike up some conversations with people in the coffee shop and make sure to maintain eye contact while I talk to them.	6
Avoid eye contact with others	Look people in the eye when I talk to them; make sure to look straight ahead and not down when I am walking.	7
Call myself names and say mean things to myself	Be kind and respectful to myself. Talk to myself like I'd talk to my best friend. Tell myself all the things I like about myself.	5

Action Urges	Opposite Actions	Helpful? (0 to 10)

MOVING FORWARD

This chapter focused on opposite action skills you can use to reduce your shame by acting in ways that are opposite to what shame makes you want to do. For emotions like shame that are not helpful, opposite action is one of the most useful sets of skills for reducing shame and lessening its hold on your life. The basic idea is to figure out what your shame makes you want to do and then just do the opposite of that. Often this means not avoiding others, not hiding who you are or your feelings, thoughts, or experiences from others, and treating yourself with kindness, compassion, respect, and love. The more you act opposite to the action urges that go along with shame, the more your shame will be reduced. These skills also have the added benefit of increasing social support, emotional intimacy, self-esteem, and self-compassion—all of which are beneficial in and of themselves. So, the next time you experience shame, figure out what it is telling you to do and then do the opposite of that, throwing yourself completely into the experience of acting opposite to those action urges.

Now that you've learned skills for managing and reducing your shame, it's time to turn your attention to skills for managing the impact of shame on your relationships. The next chapter focuses on specific strategies you can use to maintain intimacy, closeness, and well-being in relationships when you're experiencing shame.

CHAPTER 9

Managing Shame Effectively in Relationships

You might remember from previous chapters that shame is a self-conscious emotion that arises when you think about yourself and how others might perceive or evaluate you. Shame can lead to avoidance of others, make you less likely to take your needs seriously, and stop you from expressing who you are and how you feel—all of which can have a major impact on your relationships. That's why it's so important to learn how to minimize the effects of shame on your relationships and keep your relationships strong even when you're experiencing shame. The DBT skills we review in this chapter can be invaluable tools to help you do just that.

In this chapter, we will first review how shame can create problems in relationships. Then, we will discuss some of the DBT interpersonal effectiveness skills and how you can use them to overcome or prevent these problems. We hope that learning and practicing these skills will help your relationships become stronger, closer, and more fulfilling.

HOW SHAME CAN HAMPER RELATIONSHIPS AND LEAD TO LONELINESS

For many people, interpersonal situations or relationships are a common cue for feelings of shame. Researchers who study shame from an evolutionary perspective believe this emotion evolved initially to help us stay connected to our social groups or tribes. In our history as a species, it was essential to our survival to remain connected to a social group; if people were alone, there was a good chance they'd die. And, in this context, feeling shame for breaking a social norm or rule or doing something that upset others may have been helpful—it may have helped people avoid rejection and be more likely to survive.

Let's say Dan stole some extra food from the tribe and got into a fight with the tribe leader's brother. If he felt ashamed for what he had done, he'd probably try to hide it from others and keep people from finding out about it. And, if he was successful in hiding these behaviors, this would be helpful. He'd avoid getting into trouble or being kicked out of the group and sent into the wilderness alone. Somewhere along the way, though, shame seems to have become attached to people's negative, global judgments of themselves. Instead of just feeling ashamed about something they've done that may go against social norms or expectations, people feel shame about *who they are as a person*. They judge themselves as bad, flawed, inadequate, unlikeable, and so forth.

When you judge yourself, it can be easy to fall into the trap of thinking that others are judging you as well. Rather than thinking that all of your negative self-judgments are specific to you, for example, you might think that other people perceive you in the same ways you perceive yourself—as unlovable, unacceptable, and flawed. Believing that others see you this way can get in the way of your relationships and cause relationship problems.

One way that shame causes relationship problems is by prompting you to hide who you are, or to hide your identity, interests, and experiences. The problem with this is that, to have close and emotionally intimate relationships, other people need to understand and know who you are. If you hide who you are, the people close to you won't really know you. As a result, your emotional connections to others might weaken. When this happens, you might feel alone or alienated even when you're with people you're supposed to be close to. Some people refer to this as emotional loneliness (Lynch 2018). Moreover, if people don't know who you are or how you feel, they won't be able to support you when you need it.

A second way that shame causes relationship problems is by leading to avoidance of people or groups of people out of concern that they won't accept you. Avoidance of other people can lead to loneliness, isolation, and alienation from others. Being alienated from others can also lead to more shame; you might start thinking that you deserve to be alone and become even more convinced that others truly don't like or accept you. Because you're not around people, you don't get the opportunity to learn otherwise—that people seem to enjoy your company and appreciate you for who you are. The good news is that the DBT interpersonal effectiveness skills can help you work on some of the problems that shame poses for relationships. Some of the skills we'll discuss below will help you get out of the trap of avoidance, and others will help you express yourself and your needs and wants in a clear, honest, and effective way.

DBT INTERPERSONAL EFFECTIVENESS SKILLS

The DBT interpersonal effectiveness skills can help you get your needs met while maintaining strong relationships and self-respect. These skills are practical, can be used in many situations (including many not related to shame), and can help you regain a sense of mastery and self-respect in relationships. Furthermore, if you practice interpersonal effectiveness skills regularly, you might even find that your shame will diminish, you'll feel less lonely or alienated from others, and your relationships will improve.

In DBT, interpersonal effectiveness skills include many more strategies than we can cover in this chapter. We're going to focus on a few key skills that you'll find effective in reducing the impact of shame on your relationships. Here we list these strategies, and in the following sections, we describe and help you practice them and discuss how they can help with shame:

- being mindful of others in relationships

- balancing your needs with the needs of others

- identifying your relationship goals and priorities

- clearly describing to others what you want or need

- seeking what you need (by expressing your emotions, opinions, or needs in a way that enhances your relationships)

- enhancing your dignity and self-respect

Being Mindful of Others and Learning to Stop Avoiding

One of the best ways to get out of the shame/avoidance trap in relationships is to practice mindfulness of other people. This skill uses the same mindfulness skills you learned in chapter 5; you're just applying those skills to your interactions with other people. The main idea is to bring your full attention to whomever you're interacting with, fully and openly participate in the interaction, and remain in the present moment as best you can. Practicing mindfulness of others can make your social interactions more enjoyable and fulfilling, help you feel more connected with those around you, and even improve your relationships. Mindfulness is in some ways the opposite of avoidance, so practicing this skill can be a form of opposite action for urges to avoid others or hide parts of yourself due to shame (as we discussed in chapter 8). In addition, mindfulness of others is necessary before you move on to some of the other interpersonal effectiveness skills we discuss in this chapter. Before you can learn to talk and interact with people in a way that helps reduce shame, you need to start by paying attention to them.

There are several ways to practice mindfulness of others (Linehan 2015). We'll focus here on two that we think are especially helpful if you experience shame.

MINDFULLY OBSERVE AND PAY ATTENTION TO OTHER PEOPLE

Approach your time with other people with awareness, openness, and curiosity. Even if you are worried about interacting with a person or group, pay full attention to the experience. Tell yourself, *I don't really know what this'll be like, and that's fine.* Attend to your experiences with others with an open mind.

Listen to what others have to say, rather than focusing on yourself and how they might perceive you. When shame arises, it can be easy to get caught up in how you're presenting yourself, whether you're doing or saying the right thing, or how others might be thinking about you. You might get caught up in worries that others are thinking negatively about you or don't like you. When this happens, try to see those thoughts for what they are: thoughts, not facts. Let these thoughts go, and pay attention to the other person or people you're with. We know this isn't easy to do, but it becomes easier with practice.

Interact with other people with the mindset you'd use to interact with a beloved pet. When we spend time with our cats (KLG) or dog (ALC), we don't worry about what they're thinking about us. We just pay full attention to them, how cute and interesting they are, what it feels like to sit with or pet them, the interesting sounds and movements they make, and so forth. When they want to be fed, we feed them. When they want to go out, we take them out. All of our attention is focused on the experience of being with our pets and what that experience is like. And that's one reason the time we spend with our pets is so enjoyable and meaningful—we are truly immersed in that experience.

Distractions are bound to arise when we interact with other people. Our minds are used to being busy, generating thoughts, memories, and so on. These experiences can be distracting. You might find yourself getting caught up in thoughts and strong emotions (like shame) without even noticing that you're not paying attention to the person or people you're with. When your mind gets busy and your attention drifts, notice this and say to yourself, *Okay, there goes my mind again*, and gently turn your attention back to the person or people you're with.

Finally, avoid doing more than one thing at a time when you're with other people. This means that if you're out for coffee with someone, put your phone aside, avoid texting or checking your social media, and fully attend to the person in front of you. Make this person the most important person in the universe right now and give them your full attention. We think you'll discover that attending mindfully to others is also a gift to yourself.

FULLY PARTICIPATE IN THE MOMENT

Shame can sometimes make us want to step back and be a careful observer, vigilant for signs of rejection. This is like walking carefully around a swimming pool and occasionally dipping your toe into it, but never jumping in to enjoy a swim. Stepping back and simply observing, like tiptoeing around the pool, can be an avoidance behavior. As we've described earlier, avoidance behaviors often accompany shame. Sometimes the best way to counter shame is to avoid avoiding, and one way to do that is to fully participate or immerse yourself in the experience of being with others.

When you're with other people, fully participate in the present moment. Throw your whole mind and body into your interaction with the other person or people. Whether you're out for coffee, at a party, talking with someone on the phone, or helping your kids with their homework, fully participate in that activity and give it your complete attention.

Treat the conversation or interaction like you would a mindful walk or run. One of us (ALC) enjoys running in the woods, partly because of the scenery but also because he needs to remain fully engaged in and mindful of his running. If he doesn't, he'll probably trip on a rock or a root or end up on the wrong trail. Running in the woods is very different than running on a smooth, paved path; it requires full participation. Treat your time with others like you would a run in the woods.

When you're participating with others, you're bound to encounter some obstacles and distractions. Your mind will drift to other things, and shame might come along and make you feel like avoiding or withdrawing. When you find your mind drifting to other things, tell yourself, *Okay, there goes my mind again. Now I'm going to throw myself back in.*

Balancing Your Needs with Those of Others

Mindfulness is a crucial piece of the foundation of any relationship. Now that you've had some practice putting that piece in place, we're going to move on to skills that will help you start building relationships that are freer from the effects of shame.

When you struggle with shame, one of the most important things you can do in relationships is act as if your needs are important. The thoughts that accompany shame often suggest the opposite— that you're insignificant, unworthy, undeserving of good things, and that your needs, opinions, thoughts, and emotions are unimportant. If you want to reduce shame, therefore, you need to act as if your needs and experiences are important. You might recall from chapter 8 that this is one way to practice the skill of opposite action. Acting like your needs and experiences are important often involves doing the opposite of what your shame tells you to do. To get a start with this skill, consider how you're balancing your needs with those of others.

Consider the following questions and circle your response:

Do you often tell people that you're willing to do things for them even if you don't want to and it's very inconvenient for you?	Yes | No
Do you often find yourself going along with what others want to do for social events and not saying what you want to do?	Yes | No
Do you often avoid bringing up things you need, such as social support, help with something, or a change in someone else's behavior (these could be things like picking things up around your home, asking you about your day, not criticizing you so much, and so forth)?	Yes | No
Do you sometimes feel resentful, sad, or frustrated that others are not considering your needs?	Yes | No
Do you ever feel out of gas emotionally because you're doing so much for others?	Yes | No

If you answered yes to at least a few of these questions, you might have an imbalance in your relationships. Specifically, you might be prioritizing others' needs and acting as if your needs aren't important. How do you start acting like your needs are also important? One important step is to ask yourself if shame is getting in the way of asking for what you need. Here's an example:

Edwardo's Story

Edwardo is a stay-at-home dad, and his partner, Enrique, works as a management consultant. Most of the time, Edwardo finds taking care of their two young girls rewarding. Lately, however, he's starting to feel burned out. He doesn't get much of a break from shuttling the kids to and from school and recreational activities, and he's usually in charge of making dinner. Enrique often comes home late, just in time to have dinner and put the kids to bed. On the weekends, Edwardo also coordinates most of the kids' activities. He'd like to ask Enrique to help out more, but he's reluctant to do so. Enrique works nearly twelve hours a day and is often exhausted, catching up on sleep and recovering on the weekends. Another thing stopping Edwardo is that he feels some shame that he doesn't contribute to the household income and does not work outside the home. Some family members tease him about being Enrique's "wife" or not doing what a "man" should be doing. Edwardo asked himself, If I didn't feel shame about not working outside of the home and not contributing financially to our household, would I ask Enrique for more help on the weekends? The answer was yes. It was clear that shame was in his way.

Do you need something but haven't asked for it because of shame? Perhaps, like Edwardo, you'd like more help with something. Maybe you'd like someone to treat you differently, support or listen to you, take your opinions or thoughts into account, and so forth. Maybe you want a raise at work but are reluctant to ask for it. Whatever it is, first ask if shame is stopping you from seeking what you need.

Exercise 9.1: Is Shame Getting in the Way of My Needs?

What do you want or need in a relationship with someone? Describe specifically what you want or need in the space below (or download this exercise at http://www.newharbinger.com/49616). For example, Edwardo might say something like "I need more help with the kids and to get more of a break on the weekends."

What I want or need in this relationship (describe):

_____

_____

_____

Do I feel shame in this situation or relationship?	Yes | No
If I didn't feel this shame, would I ask for what I want or need?	Yes | No

Identifying Your Relationship Goals and Priorities

If shame is getting in the way of asking for what you need, the next step is to consider your priorities within the relationship. In DBT, we often say there are three key goals for any interpersonal situation: objectives, relationship, and self-respect.

OBJECTIVES

Your *objectives* are what you want or need from the other person. Consider what you'd like the other person to do or stop doing. Would you like them to listen to you, spend time with you, help you with something, provide support, treat you differently in some way, or do something for you? You've already gotten a start above in stating what you need. Now, it's time to get specific.

Describe what you'd like from that other person. Make what you need crystal clear. To do this, you have to describe what you want clearly and specifically.

_____

_____

_____

_____

_____

Let's say I (ALC) wanted someone to treat me more respectfully, and I said, "I'd really like you to treat me with more respect." Is that a specific request? Do you think the other person would know what I am talking about? Probably not. In fact, ten different people might interpret "more respect" in ten different ways.

Instead, let's say that I said, "I'd love it if you could avoid yelling at me when I ask you to do your chores." (Can you tell that ALC has teenaged sons?) Does that seem clearer? If you were the other person, would you know what I was asking of you? If so, then this is an example of a clear and specific description.

Here's Edwardo's first try at describing his objective:

I would like Enrique to help more on the weekend.

What do you think about this description? Would you know what to do if Edwardo were asking you for "more help on the weekend"? Well, if you were Enrique, you'd probably glean that "more help" means more assistance with the kids, but what kind of assistance? When? He probably wouldn't quite know what to do.

When Edwardo rewrote his objective more specifically, this is what he came up with:

I would like Enrique to take the kids to soccer on Saturday morning and cook at least one dinner on the weekend.

If Enrique were to read this, he'd have a much better idea of what Edwardo wants. If he were willing, he'd know exactly what to do to help Edwardo.

As clear as Edwardo's request was, though, something is still missing: Why is this request important to Edwardo? When you think about what you want or need, consider *why* you want or need it. Why is your objective important to you? How would the other person doing what you ask help you in some way? If you think through *why* you need your objective, you'll be ready to tell the other person why it's so important to you. Often, if people know why something is important to someone else, they are more likely to do it.

Here's what Edwardo came up with:

> Taking the kids to soccer on Saturday and cooking at least one meal would help me get some alone time to recharge. I'd also be able to go for a run on Saturday morning. You know it's important to me to stay fit, and I haven't had much time to run lately. If I could do this, I think I'd probably be less stressed out during the week.

Now it's your turn. In exercise 9.2, describe an objective. (If you prefer, download the exercise at http://www.newharbinger.com/49616.) Look at what you wrote earlier under "Describe what you'd like from that other person." Now, describe it specifically. Make it so clear that anyone would know what you're asking for.

Exercise 9.2: Describing Your Objective and Why It's Important to You

What is my objective? What do I want or need? Describe your objective in the space below, and be as clear and specific as possible.

_____

_____

_____

_____

_____

_____

Why is my objective important to me? Describe below why getting your objective is so important to you. Try to clearly state how it would help you if you were to get these needs met.

_____

_____

_____

_____

_____

_____

_____

RELATIONSHIP

Another important interpersonal priority in DBT is your relationship. DBT interpersonal effectiveness skills help you get your needs met while enhancing or maintaining good-quality relationships. When it comes to the relationship priority, therefore, ask yourself how you want the other person to feel about you and the relationship. Although no one can control how other people feel, you can interact with others in ways that strengthen your relationships, and make it more likely the other person will feel good about you and the relationship. This can also increase the chances that the other person will do what you're asking.

When Edwardo asked how he wanted Enrique to feel, he replied, "I want him to feel like I understand all of the work he does. I also want him to feel like he's not being pushed around and that I'm not trying to shirk my responsibilities or take advantage of him."

Considering your objective clarified in exercise 9.2, think about how you want the other person to feel about you and the relationship. Use exercise 9.3 here (or download the exercise at http://www .newharbinger.com/49616) to describe your relationship priority.

Exercise 9.3: Describing Your Relationship Priority

What is my relationship priority? How do I want the other person to feel about me and the relationship? How do I want my conversation with the person to influence the relationship? Describe this priority below, clearly and specifically.

_____

_____

_____

_____

_____

_____

_____

_____

SELF-RESPECT

Last but certainly not least (especially when it comes to shame), another important priority to consider is your self-respect. Ideally, getting your needs met in relationships is a win-win-win situation, in that you get what you need, the other person feels good about it, and you feel good about yourself.

In some ways, self-respect is the opposite of shame. *Self-respect* is feeling good about yourself, your choices, and your actions, and honoring your emotions, opinions, and needs. You're more likely to feel self-respect if you take your needs seriously. Therefore, acting in ways that maintain your self-respect is another way to practice opposite action (chapter 8) and combat shame.

When Edwardo considered how the situation with Enrique related to his self-respect, he came up with the following priority:

> I'd like to feel like I'm taking my feelings seriously. I do a lot to help keep the household afloat. Sometimes, I put aside things that are important to me, like my health and fitness and need for downtime. I'd like to feel like I'm standing up for myself but also being kind to Enrique.

Again, thinking about the situation you've been working on for these exercises, consider how you'd like to feel about yourself. Will asking for what you need help you feel better about yourself? Will you feel like you're taking your needs seriously—treating yourself as if you're important? Use exercise 9.4 to get some practice describing your self-respect priority. (If you prefer, download the exercise at http://www.newharbinger.com/49616.)

Exercise 9.4: Describing Your Self-Respect Priority

What is my self-respect priority? How do I want to feel about myself when or after I ask for what I need? Describe this priority below, clearly and specifically.

_____

_____

_____

_____

_____

_____

_____

Seeking What You Need

Now that you have a good idea of your priorities, it's time to figure out how to ask for what you need. The basic idea is that it's most effective to ask for what you need in a way that's clear to the other person, takes their feelings and your relationship into account, and allows you to maintain your self-respect. Sound familiar? When you ask for what you need, keep these three priorities in mind.

DEAR SKILLS

In DBT, we have skills that go with each priority. Briefly, the DEAR skills will help you achieve your objective. The GIVE skills will help you with your relationship priority. Finally, the FAST skills will help you maintain your self-respect. So, what do these skills look like?

Below, we describe the DEAR skills.

D = Describe: Describe the situation in a way that's clear to the other person. Be specific, and avoid judgmental or blaming language. When Edwardo described the situation, he said, "Enrique, I've been doing a lot of the childcare throughout the week, and I've noticed that I'm not getting much of a break on the weekend."

E = Express: Express how you feel about the situation. Use "I" statements to describe your emotions, thoughts, or opinions. Avoid judgmental language, and avoid suggesting that the other person is "making" you feel anything. Edwardo stated, "I'm starting to feel burned out. I'm more tired during the day, and I'm starting to dread having to take the kids to soccer on Saturday, when I used to enjoy it. If I had a little more downtime and could get back into my exercise and running, I think that would help recharge me."

A = Assert: Ask for what you want. Be specific and clear so the other person knows exactly what you're asking for. Avoid beating around the bush. Be confident but kind. Edwardo stated, "Could you please start taking the kids to soccer on Saturdays and cooking one of our dinners—either Saturday or Sunday?"

R = Reinforce: Tell the person ahead of time how doing what you're asking will be helpful. Think about how it might help you and them. In Edwardo's case, if Edwardo is less burned out, he'll probably be happier and more willing to go out and do fun things (the two of them used to really enjoy going to comedy clubs, but lately Edwardo hasn't felt like doing that). What's in it for Enrique to help out a little more? Well, Enrique is actually a big soccer fan and has been feeling guilty for not going to his girls' games. Also, he's always loved cooking but is working so much that he never gets to do it. Even though these activities might seem like more work to do on a weekend, they'd probably be meaningful to Enrique.

Now, give this a shot yourself. For exercise 9.5, describe the situation (D), express how you feel (E), assert (ask) your needs (A), and reinforce (R), or tell the person how doing what you're asking will be beneficial. Once you've written this out, you have a good "script" to work with and will be more prepared for when you talk with the other person about your needs. (If you prefer, download this exercise at http://www.newharbinger.com/49616.)

Exercise 9.5: Writing Out Your DEAR Script

Write out a script for what you could say to the other person, using the DEAR skills we've described. If you need help, take a look at Edwardo's example, or even ask for help from a trusted friend, counselor/therapist, or loved one.

Describe what you want and need from the other person:

_____

_____

_____

_____

_____

Express your thoughts and emotions, using "I" statements:

_____

_____

_____

_____

Assert, or ask specifically for what you want:

_____

_____

_____

_____

Reinforce, or let the person know how doing what you're asking will be helpful:

_____

_____

_____

_____

_____

GIVE SKILLS

Okay, so here is a description of the GIVE skills, which are geared toward your relationship priorities.

G = Gentle. Take a gentle approach, be kind and considerate, and avoid threats or ultimatums.

I = Interested. Express interest in the other person, their opinions, emotions, experiences, and perspectives. Be mindful when you're talking to the other person. Focus on them.

V = Validate. Convey that you understand where the other person is coming from. Show that you understand how they feel and that it makes sense that they feel this way. Avoid judging people for how they feel or what they think. All thoughts and feelings are understandable in some way, even if you don't always agree with them.

E = Easy manner. Take a soft, kind approach. Avoid criticizing, blaming, or pushing people to do things. Use humor if you can. Try to "sell" them on what you're asking for. Try to help them feel like they want to do what you're asking.

Here's an example of Edwardo's DEAR script, including the GIVE skills above:

Describe: Enrique, I love you and really appreciate all that you do for our family (**gentle, easy manner**). I've noticed that I've been doing a lot of the childcare throughout the week, and I'm not getting much of a break on the weekend either. I know you're also working so hard, doing twelve-hour days, and the last thing you probably want to do is more work around the house (**validate**).

Express: That said, I'm starting to feel burned out. I'm more tired during the day, and I'm starting to dread having to take the kids to soccer on Saturday, when I used to enjoy it. If I had a little more downtime and could get back into my exercise and running, I think that would help recharge me.

Assert: Could you please start taking the kids to soccer on Saturdays and cooking one of our dinners—either Saturday or Sunday? How would you feel about doing that? **(interested)**.

Reinforce: I'd be a lot happier and have more energy to go out with you to the comedy club, and I think you'd probably enjoy watching the girls play soccer. They're getting pretty good! **(easy manner)**.

Considering what you wrote earlier for your DEAR script, see if you could improve it by adding some of the GIVE skills, using exercise 9.6. (If you prefer, download the exercise at http://www .newharbinger.com/49616.) See if there's a way to be softer, easier, warmer, and gentler. Is there a way to add in some validation of how the other person might be feeling? Can you think of a way to express interest in the other person's perspective, even if just by asking them what they think?

Exercise 9.6: Adding Some GIVE to Your DEAR Script

If you think that your DEAR script could benefit from warming up and softening a bit by using some GIVE skills to help you reach your relationship goals, try incorporating those GIVE skills into a revised version of your DEAR script on the next page.

Describe (with GIVE):

_____

_____

_____

Express (with GIVE):

_____

_____

_____

Assert (with GIVE):

_____

_____

_____

Reinforce (with GIVE):

_____

_____

_____

Enhancing Your Dignity and Self-Respect

You're probably not surprised to hear that we also have a few skills to help you achieve your self-respect priorities. We call these the FAST skills.

FAST SKILLS

F = Fair. Be fair to yourself and others. Balance your needs with those of others. It's hard to feel much self-respect if you're walking all over others or letting them walk all over you. Edwardo kept in mind that Enrique works a lot. He didn't ask Enrique to cook dinner on both Saturday and Sunday as well as shuttle the girls to all activities on the weekend (soccer on Saturday and dance on Sundays). Instead, Edwardo asked for enough to meet his needs while also keeping in mind Enrique's need to relax and recharge.

A = no Apologies. We're not suggesting that you never apologize. If you do something that harms someone else or is not consistent with the type of person you want to be, by all means apologize. That said, some people apologize too often and for things they don't need to apologize for. This is particularly the case for people who feel a lot of shame. If you feel like many of the things you do are wrong, you'll probably apologize a lot, even when you don't need to. Here are some things you don't need to apologize for:

- how you feel

- your opinions, your wants, and your needs

- your personality

- difficult experiences you've had in life

- your emotions

- your physical or emotional pain

- your unwillingness to do things that you don't believe are right

So, Edwardo shouldn't apologize for needing a break on the weekend, feeling burned out, or asking Enrique to help. Consider when you have the urge to apologize. Before you do so, ask yourself whether this is something you really need to apologize for. Avoiding overapologizing will help you chip away at shame and maintain your self-respect.

S = Stick to values. Consistently choosing to do what you believe is right will help you maintain self-respect. We've all been in the situation where someone asks or encourages us to do something that isn't consistent with the type of person we want to be—something that doesn't fit our values. Let's say you're hanging out with a group of people, and they're gossiping negatively about someone who's not there and who you really like. Have you ever found yourself going along with it even if it made you uncomfortable? How about simply not asking the others to stop gossiping? If so, think about how you felt about yourself afterward. Doing something that goes against your values can take a toll on your self-respect.

T = Truthful. It might sound weird, but telling the truth is another way to maintain your self-respect. This doesn't mean you have to be brutally honest. One of us enjoys the TV show *Parks and Recreation*, and when someone asked the character "Donna" what she thought of a new shirt, Donna's response was "Well, it's not my favorite shirt, but it is my least favorite shirt."

That's not what we're suggesting. We're suggesting that, being honest about your wants, needs, feelings, and opinions will help you maintain your self-respect.

Let's say someone asked you to go for dinner. You've had a long day at work, and you were looking forward to some downtime with a book you just bought. You like the person and yet just don't feel up for socializing. Some people might be tempted to tell a white lie (such as to tell them you have a work meeting or something else you can't get out of) to avoid hurting the person's feelings or because they feel some embarrassment about wanting to spend time alone. As we've discussed, shame can make you feel like hiding who you are, your interests, and your preferences. Instead, being upfront about who you are, what you need (in this case, some downtime), and what you prefer can help combat shame. It's one way to practice opposite action to shame. What's more, telling people what you really want and how you feel helps them get to know you better, which strengthens your relationship.

Consider a time when you felt like shame was preventing you from saying what you really wanted to say or telling someone how you really feel. Below, write what you would like to have said if you were practicing the "T" in FAST.

_____

_____

_____

_____

_____

_____

_____

MOVING FORWARD

This chapter focused on how to keep shame from interfering with your relationships. To review, shame can have a negative effect on relationships. Shame makes you feel like avoiding people and concealing your thoughts, feelings, and needs. Avoiding people can lead to isolation, making shame worse. Hiding yourself from others prevents emotional intimacy and can lead to a sense of isolation and loneliness, even if you're around people regularly.

In this chapter, we taught you skills for being mindful of your relationships, identifying your priorities (objectives, relationship, and self-respect), and asking for what you need in ways that are effective, helpful to your relationships, and maintain your self-respect. When it comes to managing shame so that it doesn't harm your relationships, probably the two most important things to remember are (1) avoid doing what shame tells you to do (that is, avoid avoiding and hiding who you are), and (2) act as if your wants, needs, emotions, and opinions are important, while also respecting those of other people.

Congratulations! You're just about at the end of this book. Now that you've learned all of the different ways DBT skills can help you manage and cope with shame, the final chapter will focus on tying these skills together and teaching you how you can use them in combination to help you build a life free from shame.

Pulling It All Together

Congratulations! You've made it to the final chapter in this DBT skills workbook for shame! We hope that you now have a better understanding of what shame is, why it arises, and when it's most likely to arise for you, as well as all of the different skills from DBT you can use to manage shame and reduce its hold on your life.

In this final chapter, we will help you pull together some of what you've learned about coping with shame. We will start by revisiting the example of Amanda from chapter 2, focusing on how she progressed in her efforts to recover from and move beyond shame. Then, we will review some of the main points to remember about shame and give you the chance to reflect on what you've learned about your own patterns of shame. Following this, we will offer some exercises you can use to get in touch with a time (or times) when you have successfully coped with shame. Finally, we will end this chapter by returning to one of the skills we touched on in chapter 3—coping ahead. This valuable skill, along with the other skills you learned in this book, can help you break free from the hold shame has on your life.

AMANDA REVISITED

Amanda has been in therapy and learning DBT skills for about six months. She has mostly given up harming herself. She still feels like hurting herself occasionally but has only had a couple slipups (which is normal when recovering from self-harm). When she feels shame about where she is in life or about her appearance, she steps back in her mind and says, *Okay, that's shame again.* She mindfully observes the emotion for a little while and then decides what to do next. If she has time, she'll practice opposite action by actively being kind (rather than mean) to herself. She especially enjoys soothing activities like listening to music, curling up with a warm blanket, or spending time outside in nature.

Using the skill of checking the facts, Amanda will sometimes write out the situation that's bringing up shame, and then rewrite it, eliminating any negative judgments about herself and sticking to the facts. For example, words like "loser," "awkward," and "ugly" sometimes creep into her mind or show up on paper. Instead of "loser," she'll write something like "I'm disappointed that I'm still in a job where I can't use my education." Instead of "ugly," she'll write, "I still struggle to accept my body the way it is." Rather than "awkward," she'll write, "I felt anxious and out of place."

When it comes to shame in her relationships, Amanda has been a lot more open and honest with her friends (opposite action). When she feels envious of their lives, she'll tell them and start a conversation about it. She's starting to act like her needs are important. When Amanda needs someone to talk to, she'll reach out instead of avoiding and isolating herself.

Amanda is also learning to ask for the kind of help she needs. The other day, when her friend Ron kept making suggestions about jobs she could apply for, Amanda said, "I know you really want to help, and I appreciate that. Right now, though, I think I just need someone to listen. I'm not quite ready to look for new jobs, but I'm trying to cope better with the fact that I don't love this one."

Amanda still experiences shame more than she'd like to, but she's definitely noticed a reduction in her shame and she doesn't feel like it's controlling her life anymore. It's not easy, but with a lot of practice, the DBT skills she learned are coming more naturally. She sometimes uses them without even thinking about them. She feels better about herself and her relationships and more accepting of her living situation.

IMPORTANT THINGS TO REMEMBER ABOUT SHAME

To keep walking along the path to freedom from shame, as Amanda has, it's important to remember these key facts about shame:

Shame is a negative self-conscious emotion. This means that shame mostly arises when you judge or evaluate yourself as deficient, flawed, undeserving, or bad, or when you think others will think these things about you or that they will reject you.

Like all emotions, shame is made up of cognitive, physical, and behavioral components. The cognitive component usually takes the form of global, negative judgments about yourself, your characteristics, your actions, or your history. The physical component has to do with changes in your body and brain that happen when you feel shame. Sometimes you can notice these sensations, such as when you feel a change in your body temperature, heart rate, or muscle tension, or have feelings of sickness or sinking in your stomach. Other physical changes, like changes in your brain, are things you can't really sense. The behavioral component includes what you feel like doing and what you actually do when you feel shame.

Shame often makes you feel like doing things that keep shame going. Shame will often make you want to hide yourself, who you are, and your background or history from other people. The problem is that when you hide who you are or parts of yourself from other people, you don't get the opportunity to learn that most people in your life will accept you as you are, and that the parts of yourself your shame tells you are unacceptable are not. What's more, hiding parts of yourself sends a message to your brain that you have something to hide or that there's something wrong with you, which is likely to make you feel even more ashamed. Finally, shame can make you feel like avoiding people or activities that matter to you, which, in the long term, can make you feel even more isolated, lonely, miserable, and disconnected from others. That's why we're so glad the skills in this book will help you combat shame and lessen its hold on your life!

DBT SKILLS CAN HELP WITH SHAME

Although shame is a painful, persistent, and challenging emotion, we hope you've learned that DBT skills can help. Throughout this book, we've taught you many skills that you can use to manage shame. Before you can use most of these skills, however, you need to recognize that you're feeling shame. The sooner you can notice feelings of shame, the sooner you can use the other skills in this book to manage and reduce it.

Therefore, we'd like you to think about what you've learned about your own patterns of shame. You can use the exercises you completed in chapter 3 as a starting point. We are hoping you'll also use this opportunity to reflect on what you've learned about your experience of shame since you completed those exercises. As you've read this book and learned more about your shame, do you have a better sense of what shame feels like for you as well as the early signs that you're experiencing shame? Think about the new information you've learned and write it on the next page.

REFLECTING ON A SUCCESS STORY WITH DBT SKILLS FOR SHAME

Now that you've reflected on what you've learned about your experience and patterns of shame, another helpful step to take as you finish this book is to describe a success story of coping with shame. When you struggle with mood difficulties or challenging emotions like shame, sometimes negative events and memories come to mind easily. You might remember when you forgot to use skills, didn't cope as well as you would have liked, got swallowed up by shame all evening and avoided people, and so on. Positive experiences of coping with your shame effectively and memories of times when you coped well might not arise quite as easily. Yet, it's crucial to learn from your experiences of coping effectively with shame. Reflecting on such experiences can help you identify DBT skills that you might want to remember and use again later.

Use exercise 10.1 to describe a time when you experienced strong shame and coped with it effectively. See if you can think of a time when you felt proud of yourself for how you coped. Many people think that pride is the opposite of shame; it's hard to feel both shame and pride at the same time. Once you've written down times when you felt proud of how you coped, you can always return to this description (and maybe describe some more) and hopefully get in touch with how you felt. You'll also have a reminder of what worked in the past and what might work in the future.

Before you get started with this exercise, here's an example of Molly's description. The DBT skills she used are noted in bold in square brackets.

I felt anxious, but I agreed to meet Nigel at his place for a get-together with his new girl-friend and some of her friends [**opposite action to anxiety**]. Knowing that I often feel shame around new people, I tried to make sure I got a good night's sleep the night before and didn't skip any meals that day [**reducing vulnerability to shame**]. When I skip meals, my emo-tions get a lot more intense, and I tend to be more stressed out. Therefore, I wanted to be sure I wasn't entering the situation in a state where I'd be vulnerable to having intense shame. I worried that I didn't have any flattering clothes to wear but just decided to put on what I felt most comfortable in and show up confidently [**opposite action**]. But even when I thought about showing up, I started to feel my telltale signs of shame—that sinking feeling in my stomach, flushed cheeks, feelings of choking. I noticed these physical sensations and practiced accepting that they were there, even though I didn't like them [**mindfulness**]. I got ready mindfully, got in my car, and turned on some good music [**distraction**]. When I got there, I noticed thoughts like "I'm not as good/attractive as these people." "Why are they all so much better than me?" "What's wrong with me?" I stepped back in my mind and told myself, "These are thoughts, not facts" [**mindfulness of thoughts**]. I reminded myself that judging myself is just fuel for shame. I told myself, "I don't even know these people. There's no reason to think they're any better than me or that anyone is any better than anyone else, for that matter. I'm Nigel's best friend, and I'm an important part of his life. I'm here to get to know his girlfriend and maybe her friends and have a good time" [**checking the facts**]. During dinner and a game we all played together, I did my best to throw myself into talking and playing the game [**mindfully participating**]. Although things were going pretty well, after the game, I noticed I wanted to leave. Nigel asked me if I could stay a bit longer, which was nice, but I really didn't want to. I wanted to go home and relax; I had to get up early for work the next day. I told Nigel that I'd had a great time, but was feeling like I needed some downtime, and that I'd like to take off soon [**interpersonal effectiveness skills**]. I got home and felt pretty exhausted. All that coping took some work! I took a warm bath and went to bed [**self-soothing, self-care**]. I felt proud of myself for going, having a good time, and leaving when I wanted to. My shame was probably at a 7 out of 10 when I got to the party but around a 2 out of 10 when I was leaving. Much better than parties in the past!

Exercise 10.1: Describing a Time When You Coped Well with Shame

Below, please describe a time when you coped well with shame. Describe the situation you were in, your shame and how intense it was, what you did to cope with it, and how it worked out for you. See if you can describe why what you did was so effective. Also, see if you can identify some of the DBT skills that you used, as we have for Molly's description. (If you prefer, you can download this exercise at http://www .newharbinger.com/49616.)

Description:

_____

_____

_____

_____

_____

_____

_____

_____

_____

_____

_____

COPING AHEAD

There's just one more skill we want to review before we finish up: the DBT skill of coping ahead. As we discussed in chapter 3, *coping ahead* can help you practice and prepare for stressful situations. This skill involves thinking ahead about a situation where you might experience shame and planning how you'll cope effectively with your shame if it arises. You can think of this as a form of mental practice for how you'll cope. In Molly's case, she might start by thinking about the next get-together she might go to, since those tend to elicit shame for her. Then, she would imagine herself getting through that get-together effectively, using skills to manage shame.

Practicing like this in your imagination can sometimes be almost as good as practicing in real life. In fact, athletes often do this: they practice skills they'll need to use in an upcoming game, like soccer, hockey, tennis, and so forth. One of us (ALC) practices martial arts, and before tests, he has sometimes imagined himself performing the different moves he'll be tested on.

Exercise 10.2: Coping Ahead with Shame

Here are some instructions for coping ahead with shame. (An audio track of these instructions is available at http://www.newharbinger.com/49616.)

Step 1: Find a comfortable and relaxing place to be, ideally with no distractions. You might decide that you want to do this exercise seated in a comfortable, relaxed position, lying down, or even walking. (Some people find it easier to do this kind of thing while pacing or moving.)

Step 2: Think about a future situation in which you might feel mild to moderate shame. Don't practice this skill the first time with intense shame. It's a new skill, so it helps to practice with mild or moderate shame and work your way up to more intense shame.

Step 3: Take a few minutes to practice some breathing. One helpful way to do this is to try to breathe from your diaphragm. Put your hand on your abdomen, and try to breathe slowly but comfortably in such a way that your hand moves up and down. Try to avoid shallow breathing where you breathe in and out from your chest. If you notice your shoulders going up and down, try to relax them (you're probably chest breathing if your shoulders are moving).

Step 4: Once you feel fairly calm and centered, imagine yourself in a situation where you might feel some shame. Make a mental note or write down your level of shame on a scale from 0 (none at all) to 10 (extreme shame).

Step 5: If you feel comfortable doing this, close your eyes and imagine yourself in that situation. Really try to imagine the situation as if it's happening right now. Try to bring to mind the sights, sounds, thoughts, and feelings that you would have in that situation.

Step 6: Now, imagine yourself coping well with that situation, using some of the DBT skills you learned in this book. For example, you might start by imagining the skill of mindfully observing your shame cues. Next, you could imagine describing to yourself that shame is coming up. Imagine how you'd interact with people (if people are there), maybe using opposite action by having a confident body posture, making eye contact, and being open when talking to these people (and avoiding hiding or leaving the situation). You might imagine yourself successfully resisting the type of coping that tends to make things worse, such as self-damaging behavior, drinking, or using drugs. Maybe you'll imagine using checking the facts to reframe judgmental thoughts about yourself. Whatever skills apply best to your situation, give those skills a try in your mind.

Step 7: Try this for about five to ten minutes, and once you're done, make a mental or actual note of your level of shame again from 0 to 10. Also, if you have time, write down some of the skills that you practiced in your imagination so you'll be more likely to remember them later.

Step 8: Finally, return to the diaphragmatic breathing we mentioned in step 3. Do this for about five minutes. You can repeat all of these steps as many times as you wish. As with learning any new skill, practice and repetition can be crucial.

After you've used the skill of coping ahead, it can be helpful to take some time to reflect on the skills you practiced in your mind. We're confident that, if you use coping ahead to practice DBT skills before you get into situations that tend to elicit shame for you, you'll be better prepared to use your skills in those situations and you'll probably get through those situations with less shame. Further, instead of being hijacked by shame, you'll be able to focus on what's most important to you, whether that's having a fun and fulfilling time with others or simply being at peace with yourself.

MOVING FORWARD TOWARD FREEDOM FROM SHAME

Congratulations, you've reached the end of our workbook on shame! We hope that you've found many of the skills in this book to be helpful tools in your journey toward a life free from shame.

With any difficult problem or emotion, you'll probably find that there are times when you feel like you're taking two steps forward and one step back. There will be times when you'll feel intense shame; there's really no way around that. Remember, though, that you're much better equipped now to deal with that shame. Even if you slip back into old patterns, lapse into behaviors (such as harmful coping methods) that just make things worse for yourself, or say or do things you later regret, these are just lapses. You've learned new skills that you can't unlearn, and you can always get back on track and use them effectively in the next difficult situation.

We sincerely wish you all the best and hope you continue to find our book helpful as a resource for coping with shame.

Acknowledgments

I am grateful for an amazing group of friends, family, and colleagues. Kim and I have known each other for over twenty-two years now, starting when we were both applying for predoctoral clinical psychology internships and we connected over email about shared research interests. This is the seventh book we've written together. Although we don't get to see each other very often, I consider Kim to be one of my dearest friends, and writing with her has always been delightful. This book came along at a challenging time for both of us, but we managed to write it anyway, and I feel proud of our work. Over the past few years, I've discovered friends I didn't realize I had, and I'd like to express my sincere appreciation for their support. I also appreciate all of my incredible supervisors, mentors, and teachers over the years, whose voices I still hear whenever I write about DBT or psychology stuff. The steadfast, warm, caring, and attentive support of my wife, Katherine, has seen me through so many things in life. I'd like to also express appreciation for my family, my two sons, and our dog, Charlie, who is a new addition to the family since our last book. Short breaks to hang out with Charlie have given me the comfort and energy to get through the home stretch.

—Alexander L. Chapman

I am incredibly grateful to my dear friend, colleague, and coauthor, Alex Chapman, for our ongoing collaboration. It's been a few years since we've written a book together, and I had forgotten just how much I enjoy the process. I look forward to continued collaborations on other such projects in the future. I am also incredibly grateful to Catharine Meyers at New Harbinger for her commitment to this book. This book would not have been possible without her dedication to the project and persistence in encouraging us to write it. Without that, I would have missed out on what has been an incredibly rewarding and meaningful experience. I would also like to thank the team at New Harbinger for their editorial assistance throughout this process.

I am also grateful to my family for all of their love and support. First, to my parents, Linda and Dave, for their unwavering support, unconditional love, and steadfast validation throughout my life. They provided the foundation for everything I've accomplished in my career. I am also eternally grateful to Sadie and Lily for joining our family at the perfect time and bringing us so much love, joy, and peace. A special thanks to Sadie in particular for being such a perfect writing companion and making the writing process even more enjoyable. Finally, I will always be most grateful to my husband, partner, and best friend, Matt Tull, for everything he does to support, sustain, comfort, and assist me in life and work. His willingness to care for me and his consummate emotional, physical, and culinary support make everything possible and my life far better. I am extraordinarily grateful to share my life with him.

—Kim L. Gratz

References

Bourne, E. J. 1995. *The Anxiety and Phobia Workbook*. 2nd ed. Oakland, CA: New Harbinger Publications.

Chapman, A. L., K. L. Gratz, and M. T. Tull. 2011. *The Dialectical Behavior Therapy Skills Workbook for Anxiety: Breaking Free from Worry, Panic, PTSD, and Other Anxiety Symptoms*. Oakland, CA: New Harbinger Publications.

Drapalski, A. L., A. Lucksted, P. B. Perrin, J. M. Aakre, C. H. Brown, B. R. DeForge, and J. E. Boyd. 2013. "A Model of Internalized Stigma and Its Effects on People with Mental Illness." *Psychiatric Services* 64 (3): 264–69.

Epstein, L. J., D. Kristo, P. J. Strollo Jr., N. Friedman, A. Malhotra, S. P. Patil et al. 2009. "Clinical Guidelines for the Evaluation, Management, and Long-Term Care of Obstructive Sleep Apnea in Adults." *Journal of Clinical Sleep Medicine* 5 (3): 263–76.

Lewis, H. B. 1971. *Shame and Guilt in Neurosis*. New York: International Universities Press.

Lewis, M., M. W. Sullivan, C. Stanger, and M. Weiss. 1989. "Self Development and Self-Conscious Emotions." *Child Development* 60 (1): 146–56.

Linehan, M. M. 1993a. *Cognitive Behavioral Treatment of Borderline Personality Disorder*. New York: Guilford Press.

———. 1993b. *Skills Training Manual for Treating Borderline Personality Disorder*. 1st ed. New York: Guilford Press.

———. 2015. *DBT Skills Training Manual*. 2nd ed. New York: Guilford Press.

———. 2020. *Building a Life Worth Living: A Memoir*. New York: Random House.

Lynch, T. R. 2018. *Radically Open Dialectical Behavior Therapy: Theory and Practice for Treating Disorders of Overcontrol*. Oakland, CA: Context Press.

Lysaker, P. H., D. Roe, and P. T. Yanos. 2006. "Toward Understanding the Insight Paradox: Internalized Stigma Moderates the Association Between Insight and Social Functioning, Hope, and Self-Esteem Among People with Schizophrenia Spectrum Disorders." *Schizophrenia Bulletin* 33 (1): 192–99.

Nummenmaa, L., E. Glerean, R. Hari, and J. K. Hietanen. 2013. "Bodily Maps of Emotions." *Proceedings of the National Academy of Sciences* 111 (2): 646–51.

Rizvi, S. L., and M. M. Linehan. 2005. "The Treatment of Maladaptive Shame in Borderline Personality Disorder: A Pilot Study of 'Opposite Action.'" *Cognitive and Behavioral Practice* 12 (4): 437–47.

Rössler, W. 2016. "The Stigma of Mental Disorders: A Millennia-Long History of Social Exclusion and Prejudices." *EMBO Reports* 17 (9): 1250–53.

Schoenleber, M., and H. Berenbaum. 2012. "Shame Regulation in Personality Pathology." *Journal of Abnormal Psychology* 121 (2): 433–46.

Simbayi, L. C., S. Kalichman, A. Strebel, A. Cloete, N Henda, and A. Mqeketo. 2007. "Internalized Stigma, Discrimination, and Depression Among Men and Women Living with HIV/AIDS in Cape Town, South Africa." *Social Science & Medicine* 64 (9): 1823–31.

Shunryu, S. 1970. *Zen Mind, Beginner's Mind.* New York: Weatherhill.

Tangney, J. P., and R. L. Dearing. 2002. *Shame and Guilt.* New York: Guilford Press.

———, and J. L. Tracy. 2012. "Self-Conscious Emotions." In *Handbook of Self and Identity*, edited by M. R. Leary and J. P. Tangney. 2nd ed. (pp. 446–78). New York: Guilford Press.

———, P. Wagner, C. Fletcher, and R. Gramzow. 1992. "Shamed into Anger? The Relation of Shame and Guilt to Anger and Self-Reported Aggression." *Journal of Personality and Social Psychology* 62 (4): 669–75.

Waugh, O. C., D. G. Bryne, and M. K. Nicholas. 2014. "Internalized Stigma in People Living with Chronic Pain." *The Journal of Pain* 15 (5): 550.e1–10.

West, M. L., P. T. Yanos, S. M. Smith, D. Roe, and P. H. Lysaker. 2011. "Prevalence of Internalized Stigma Among Persons with Severe Mental Illness." *Stigma Research and Action* 1 (1): 54–59.

Alexander L. Chapman, PhD, RPsych, is professor, director of clinical training, and coordinator of the clinical science area in the psychology department at Simon Fraser University in Canada, as well as a registered psychologist and president of the DBT Centre of Vancouver. Chapman directs the Personality and Emotion Research Lab, where he studies the role of emotion regulation in borderline personality disorder (BPD), self-harm, impulsivity, as well as other related issues. His research has been funded by major grants from the Canadian Institutes of Health Research. Chapman has received the Young Investigator's Award from the National Education Alliance for Borderline Personality Disorder (NEABPD), the Canadian Psychological Association's Scientist Practitioner Early Career Award, and a Career Investigator award from the Michael Smith Foundation for Health Research.

Chapman has coauthored twelve books for consumers and clinicians. Board certified in cognitive behavioral therapy (CBT) (Canadian Association for Cognitive and Behavioral Therapies) and dialectical behavior therapy (DBT) (DBT-Linehan Board of Certification), Chapman cofounded a psychology practice focused on DBT, and regularly gives workshops and presentations to clinicians and community groups both nationally and internationally. He also has been practicing martial arts and mindfulness meditation for many years, and enjoys cooking, reading, outdoor activities, and spending time with his family.

Kim L. Gratz, PhD, is a senior clinical quality manager and clinical lead of the DBT program at Lyra Health. She also maintains an appointment in the department of psychology at the University of Toledo, where she previously served as professor and chair. Gratz directs the Personality and Emotion Research Lab, where her laboratory and treatment outcome research focus on the role of emotion dysregulation in BPD, suicidal and nonsuicidal self-injury, and substance use, as well as the intergenerational transmission of BPD-relevant mechanisms. Gratz has received multiple awards for her research on personality disorders and self-injury, including the Young Investigator's Award from the NEABPD in 2005, the Mid-Career Investigator Award from the North American Society for the Study of Personality Disorders in 2015, and the President's Award for Excellence in Creative and Scholarly Activity from the University of Toledo in 2022. She was also recognized by the University of Toledo Catharine S. Eberly Center for Women as an Influential Woman (Innovator) for her research on BPD, self-injury, and emotion regulation. She has been continuously funded since 2003 (with continuous federal funding as principal investigator from 2008-2020), and has authored more than 240 peer-reviewed publications and seven books on BPD, self-injury, and DBT.

MORE BOOKS from
NEW HARBINGER PUBLICATIONS

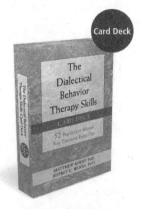

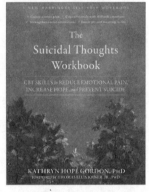

Did you know there are **free tools** you can download for this book?

Free tools are things like **worksheets**, **guided meditation exercises**, and **more** that will help you get the most out of your book.

You can download free tools for this book—whether you bought or borrowed it, in any format, from any source—from the New Harbinger website. All you need is a NewHarbinger.com account. Just use the URL provided in this book to view the free tools that are available for it. Then, click on the "download" button for the free tool you want, and follow the prompts that appear to log in to your NewHarbinger.com account and download the material.

You can also save the free tools for this book to your **Free Tools Library** so you can access them again anytime, just by logging in to your account! Just look for this button on the book's free tools page. ➜

+ Save this to my free tools library

If you need help accessing or downloading free tools, visit **newharbinger.com/faq** or contact us at **customerservice@newharbinger.com**.